Civil Service College
Handbook/number 23

CU00811907

Understanding
Published Accounts

Paul Mower
(Robson Rhodes)

LONDON
HER MAJESTY'S STATIONERY OFFICE

ISBN 0 11 630446 4

Contents

Introduction

The style of accounts seen to-day and the information they contain have evolved via company law, standards set by accountancy bodies and developing styles of best practice. It is something of a compromise between interests which may conflict. Firstly there is the company's natural reluctance to release certain information, particularly in relation to profit margins, which is felt could harm its trading position vis à vis its competitors or in some cases the public generally.

On the other hand users such as shareholders, commentators, unions, potential investors and lenders, often feel that the information which they presently receive from published accounts is inadequate for their varying needs. This is particularly so in relation to analysis of costs, gross profits and how those profits are derived from the different segments of the company. The only users of accounts who have this extra information available are management themselves and the Inland Revenue who can request this on a confidential basis.

The law and the accountancy profession have historically represented the users in setting disclosure requirements for accounts to satisfy users' needs and yet not impose an unreasonable burden on the companies. In so far as the result is a compromise it has meant an end product which does not totally satisfy anyone.

Despite shortcomings in accounts, it serves no purpose for any users to throw up their hands and dismiss published accounts as not meeting their needs, as they usually represent the only information available. One has to try to understand the information given, be aware of certain shortcomings, and from that build up a picture of the company's fortunes.

Accounts are a vehicle for giving the users information which they require for different purposes to assess the financial performance and the current strengths and stability of the company within the market. Neither conventional accounts nor accounts adjusted for inflation attempt to value the business either in terms of what it would be worth if its constituent assets were broken up and sold or if the business were sold as a going concern. However the varying users want at least enough information to be able to estimate such values for themselves.

Conventional accounts are drawn up on what is termed the historical cost convention which broadly means all transactions being recorded at their original cost when the transaction was made. Such accounts do not attempt to amend the value of these transactions for the effect of inflation or to upgrade the collective value of the constituent assets when they are combined to form a business which is a going concern.

The reasons why such an approach would not be practical are discussed further later on in the text, but once again certain users want sufficient information to form their own opinions.

In the short term there may be a source of confusion in that published annual reports will, in many cases, contain two sets of accounts purporting to give information on the same business, which show quite different results i.e. conventional and inflation adjusted accounts.

Inflation adjusted accounts are required for all companies listed on the stock exchange and large unlisted companies for accounting periods commencing after 1 January 1980—a later chapter sets out the principles of inflation adjusted accounts and their relationship to conventional accounts. The form of inflation adjusted accounts which has been adopted in the UK records these

2

same transactions on the basis of current values. This is not a contradiction and, provided the basis for the figures is understood, the presentation of the additional current cost data should inform rather than confuse the user.

Because historical cost accounts are at present still the prevalent convention, the substantial part of this handbook has been structured around these. However the principal concepts and accounting problems set out apply substantially to accounts generally under whatever convention they are prepared. The approach to examining critically profitability, performance generally, liquidity and financial structure, as explained for historical accounts can all be viewed equally in current value terms and will normally give much more meaningful results.

The purpose of this booklet is to assist the user in understanding his or her way round a typical annual report, the significance and limitations of the information they contain and generally how to interpret that information and reach some broad conclusions.

The approach in this handbook is as follows:

—To explain briefly some of the principles by which the figures in accounts are prepared

—To explain the contents of the annual report generally

—To walk through a typical set of published accounts. The example of the accounts of the Rank Organisation Limited has been reproduced by the kind permission of the company in the Appendix and the relevant chapter is structured to take the reader through these with explanations

—To explain some of the areas in accounts where, due to the flexibility or complexity of permitted accounting policies, the user may find it hardest to assess the full implications of the figures produced

—To identify some of the key figures and relationships of figures in the accounts that the user should examine

3

—To look at the development of accounts adjusted for inflation, the significance of the figures they produce and how these can be interpreted

—To explain briefly some other forms of financial statements which are becoming more common in annual reports.

Principles Used in
Preparing Accounts

Fundamental concepts

There are numerous accounting requirements and principles which govern the preparation of any particular set of accounts but common to all are four fundamental concepts, which are:

The concept of consistency

The concept of prudence

The going concern concept

The accruals and matching concepts.

There has been much written about these in accounting literature but the purpose here is not to discuss the academic side of these concepts but rather the implications, particularly with regard to prudence, which they can have for an understanding and interpretation of the accounts.

The concept of consistency

This is perhaps the most self-explanatory of the fundamental concepts. Whilst accounting policies can change over a number of years, the general principle is to retain consistency and change only when, in the circumstances, the new policy appears to be a significant improvement. When such a change does occur the company will generally restate the comparative figures in the accounts to ensure that consistency still prevails.

The concept of prudence

The concept of prudence generally manifests itself in the form that when in doubt you assume the worst. Also where trading assets become worth less than their carrying value in the books, this must be reflected in the accounts but where they are worth more no adjustment is made.

Consider the following examples. A company enters into two forward contracts prior to the accounting year end. Calculations may show that if these contracts were closed at the date of preparation of the accounts one would show a loss of £10,000 and the other a profit of £50,000. The accounts do not include a £40,000 resulting profit on forward contacts, nor do they even leave out any profit or loss on forward contracts on the basis that unrealised losses are more than covered by unrealised profits. The profit and loss account for the current year will in fact recognise the £10,000 loss but ignore the £50,000 profit.

Consider also a company with two categories of stock, A and B, of total cost £100,000 and £50,000 respectively and that the company shows stock in the accounts at the lower of cost and net realisable value, which is by far the most common basis used. If the net realisable value of the stocks were £80,000 for A and £90,000 for B, the value that will be given in the accounts is not £170,000 being the total net realisable value nor £150,000 being the total cost which is lower. It is £130,000 being the worst of both worlds taking £80,000 as the lowest basis for A plus £50,000 as the lowest for B. The purpose of these examples is not to attack the prudence concept. There is a strong argument for assuming the worst in the construction of accounts—better perhaps to plan on this basis and find things turning out better. However, the user must be fully aware of the implications. Accounts are drawn up on a prudent basis and this means a deliberate bias as they are not even attempting to give a balanced picture. This is one reason why the internal management accounts are usually different from the published accounts because the former are generally based on the most likely outcome rather than the most prudent one.

The going concern concept

This concept is the assumption, in the absence of evidence to the contrary, that the business will continue for the foreseeable future. The accounts assign figures to the assets, liabilities, income and expenses in the light of this assumption, and not in the quite different light which would be cast on them were the company to be approaching liquidation or other cessation.

Consider plant and machinery, for example. If the company were to be about to cease, it would clearly be appropriate to show this at its net realisable value i.e. the price for which it could be sold second hand. As plant and machinery tends to be specialised for any particular business this value is usually relatively low.

However such a pessimistic view is not appropriate as it is not envisaged that the plant will in fact be sold and it is therefore retained at its original cost less depreciation charged to date. (This is of course assuming that the accounts are prepared on a historical cost convention, which is further considered below).

The accruals and matching concepts

These concepts require that revenue and costs are accounted for when earned or incurred, not simply when money is received or paid. The concept further means that revenues should as far as possible be matched in the same period as the costs to which they relate. Therefore if for example only three quarters of rent are actually paid in one year, simply because the final quarter was settled just after the year end, the profit and loss account is still charged with a full four quarters and a creditor is set up for the last quarter. This is because all of that rent actually relates to the current year and it would distort the profit and loss account to include only three quarters this year, and then, as a result, five quarters next year merely because an invoice was a few days late being settled. Similarly if any invoices are paid in advance, all or part of these amounts are carried forward (in debtors) at the year end and then included in the profit and loss account next year, which is the year to which they relate. Identifying the correct year to which income and expenses relate can be much harder to employ in practice than it sounds in theory, particularly in cases such as long term contracts or leases when it is by no means self-evident exactly when the revenue actually is earned.

Accounting Conventions

The four concepts above will apply in normal cases for all accounts and they are principles which will apply whatever conventions of costs and valuations are adopted. The most well known is of course the historical cost convention which has been with us for many years and, until recently, was the only basis on which the published accounts were produced. It simply means that costs and income should be initially recorded and subsequently accounted for at their historical monetary amounts i.e. the cash amounts actually paid or received. A piece of machinery purchased is shown at its original cost less the annual depreciation charged to date. The valuation is in fact somewhat arbitrary. It neither purports to reflect the actual economic value of the machine to the business, nor does it reflect what it would actually cost to replace the machine today with a new, or equivalent secondhand one. Equally when an item of stock which has been held for a period of time is sold, under the historical cost convention, the original cost of the stock is written off in the profit and loss account. This is however not the true cost to the business because if the stock has been held for a period then its cost in real terms is higher as, due to inflation, it will cost more to replace it with new stock to sell. These are some of the factors which are incorporated in the current cost accounting (CCA) convention.

After much debate in the 1970s CCA has emerged as the convention which is thought to be a meaningful approach in a time when historical costs become almost immediately outdated by inflation. It does produce a profit and loss account in which the costs matched against sales do approximate to a measure of the value of the resources consumed.

The present situation is that basic CCA accounts are required to be produced in addition to the full historical cost accounts by many companies. In time historical cost accounts may be phased out but this is likely to be some way off. Almost everyone admits to

the vast limitations of the historical cost accounts but it is a convention which has been around for a long time and, as the debate
on the possible alternatives produced many possibilities there is
perhaps reluctance at this stage to do away with a convention
which for all its inherent weaknesses is widely understood and its
shortcomings known. Historical cost accounts remain those
which form the basis for computing tax. When CCA becomes
more widely understood and used, its advantages over historical
cost accounting will probably cause it to become the prevalent
convention.

In the short term the very existence of two sets of accounts
produced side by side, both purporting to show the financial
position and results of the company may serve to confuse rather
than inform many users. There is no doubt that as of to-day
historical cost accounts with full supporting notes are still the
main core of the annual reports produced by most companies and
therefore it is these which this booklet will concentrate on
although a later chapter does deal exclusively with CCA accounts.

Sources of disclosure and accounting rules
The actual constraints on accounting treatment and what
accounting information companies should disclose come from
many sources. First and foremost there are the Companies Acts
of 1948 and 1967. The very fact that these were produced some
years ago and the different users of accounts have changed in that
time is worth noting. The Companies Act of 1976 did not deal
with disclosure in accounts at all. The 1980 Companies Act has
only limited content with regard to new disclosure—principally in
the area of information on director's and officer's benefits and
interests. In the future there will be the general impact on UK
disclosure of EEC Directives which are substantially embodied in
the new Companies Act 1981.

The other major area of constraint is Statements of Standard
Accounting Practice (SSAP) issued by the Consultative Committee
of Accountancy Bodies. These requirements are not legally
binding on companies as such, however members of the relevant
accounting institutes who assume responsibilities in respect of

financial accounts, be they company officers or auditors, are expected to observe these standards. Where they are not followed, they must disclose and explain any significant departures from them. Hence, if a company wishes to avoid reference in the audit report these must be complied with. There are also international accounting standards which are generally compatible with our domestic standards.

Where a company is listed there are further Stock Exchange requirements for disclosure to be met. Finally there is an overall constraint, which is hard to measure, being the emerging best practice and tide of opinion. If a trend begins to emerge for disclosure of particular accounting information there becomes some pressure for other companies to follow suit both to be progressive and to avoid raising suspicion with users as to whether this particular item represents a problem with the company.

Conclusion

Having briefly explained the concepts and conventions used and the sources of rules on disclosure and accounting treatment, an important concluding point to make is that, despite this framework, accountancy is not an exact science. This is because accounts consist not only of a summary of the cash transactions made by a company in a year but also of estimates of the value of unpaid liabilities, the value of unsold stock, the extent of future losses, the length of time that fixed assets will be in use (and hence their depreciation rates) and many more. These are reached by judgement and as they are judgement the answers will not always be the same. However, the problem can go further. Because accounting is not an exact science it offers a degree of creativity by following the letter rather than the spirit of the law and accounting standards. Some companies may seek disclosure and accounting treatment to show results in the most favourable way, nevertheless meeting all legal and professional requirements. It would be easy to take a view that it reflects badly on the persons who drafted the Companies Acts and the Statements of Standard Accounting practice that such a degree of flexibility should exist. Such a view is generally not fair. It would be relatively easy to draft legislation and standards which were inflexible. However it is likely that this would produce more misleading results as one particular set of rules may work well for a particular type of business but produce grossly unrealistic accounts in another case. The results in the United States, where standards are generally much less flexible, do nothing to indicate that this makes for easier interpretation. What is important, if flexibility is allowed, is that the policies adopted are disclosed so that the user can form his own opinion as to whether they are likely to produce realistic results and whether those results can be reasonably compared to a similar business, which may have followed different policies.

The General Content of an Annual Report

Chairman's (or President's) review
This is usually the first item found in the annual report. It is an area of the annual report which has virtually no prescribed constraints as to its content and, within reason, the chairman can say whatever he wishes about the company's performance in the year and often a little political comment as well. It is usually very readable, full of broad comment and written in a style to lift or maintain the spirits of all concerned with the company.

In terms of assessing and interpreting the accounting results of the company, it is of general background interest.

Notice of meeting
The chairman's review is usually followed, sometimes preceded, by the notice of the forthcoming annual general meeting the purpose of which generally includes the approval by the shareholders of the accounts. Most of the items included in the notice are relatively formal shareholders' matters such as approval of the dividend, election of directors and appointment of auditors.

General information
This heading can cover just about anything, but it is used here broadly to cover all other information included in the annual report which is not part of the audited accounts or the director's

report. It tends to be presented in the package ahead of the audited accounts. Like the chairman's review, there is no prescribed content or constraints as to what is included and so most of this should be treated as useful background information. It frequently includes a 'Summary of the Year' which consists of certain important figures from the accounts summarised in isolation. This may take the form of a columnised summary of the results of a number of years; a five year summary is in fact a Stock Exchange recommendation for listed companies. This information can be of great value to the user but it needs to be treated with some caution if the information does not seem to give the complete picture. For example, trends of sales, earnings and profit retained for the year can be very misleading if trends of capital employed and numbers of shares etc., are not also given (more on this later). Much of the content of this area is basically pure advertising, including glossy pictures of happy employees, products in use and products for the future. There is considerable scope for charts and graphs and often some financial information analysing certain aspects of the company's results and assets over the different products and activities. Remember that any financial information provided here is not part of the audited accounts. That does not mean that this is not useful and accurate information but bear in mind that all of this material can be included or excluded at the discretion of the directors so it may be presented in such a way as to show the company in the most favourable light. Naturally it would be naive to imply that this does not, to some extent, apply to the audited accounts as well but at least these are subject to an independent examination which seeks to establish that the accounts give 'a true and fair view'.

Some companies do actually build this information concerning different products and activities (segmented information) into the main body of the audited accounts which is obviously more desirable for the user. Certain other financial statements, although not strictly required, may also be included amongst this general information or, less frequently, within the main body of the accounts. Examples of these are value added statements and employment statements which are discussed later in this handbook.

13

Directors' report

The information found here is much more detailed and specific than that found in the chairman's review because the Companies Acts 1948 and 1967 stipulate much of the information which must be disclosed in this report. Of course, the styles of these reports vary considerably. Some are just a statement of the minimum information required which includes some basic analysis of the turnover and profitability of different classes of business of the company. On the other hand, examples are seen where they are lengthy, discursive and contain considerable detail.

As the contents of this report, like the accounts, are considerably dictated by law, it is to all intents and purposes part of the accounts. As we will see, the auditor's report specifically does not include an opinion on the contents of the directors' report. However in practical terms the auditors will always review the content of the directors' report as representations made in this report by the directors which were inconsistent with the main body of the accounts would have to affect the opinion of the auditors on those accounts.

The accounts

Usually, these are to be found as the final part of the package. The word 'accounts' loosely covers a series of financial statements and referenced notes, which have been subjected to a full independent statutory audit. As explained, the other sections of the total annual report may contain some financial statements, analysis and written explanation of the company's activities, so it may not be clear at first sight which pages constitute the audited accounts. To find this, the user should turn to the auditors report which will begin 'We have audited the accounts set out on pages to ....'. Usually the total number of pages referred to is less than a third of the total package.

As it is the accounts themselves which this booklet will deal with, it is worth examining exactly what this term comprises.

14

Content of the Accounts

Group (consolidated) accounts generally

This handbook is designed to assist in the understanding of published accounts. In most cases this involves companies which are part of a group structure, i.e. a holding company which itself owns sufficient shares to have a controlling interest in one or more companies, termed subsidiaries, who in turn may have a controlling interest in other companies. A controlling interest broadly means more than 50 per cent of the ordinary share capital.

In these circumstances accounts are prepared for the group as a whole. In simplified terms, consider a group which consists of a holding company which holds 60 per cent of the shares of a subsidiary. The group profit will consist of the whole profit of the holding company plus 60 per cent of that of the subsidiary. The group balance sheet will basically be an addition of the assets and the liabilities of the holding company and the subsidiary less the share of these assets and liabilities which are attributable to the shareholders outside the group, i.e. the holders of the other 40 per cent of the shares in the subsidiary. This is termed the minority interest and it is expressed as one figure, being their net share of assets and liabilities, rather than deducting their share from each individual asset and liability. This is a simplification of the accounting entries involved, but this broad understanding is needed at this stage to appreciate the different financial statements which need to be included in the accounts as a whole.

For the purposes of illustration the accounts for the year to 31 October 1980 of the Rank Organisation Limited are reproduced in the Appendix at the end of this booklet. They were chosen as an example of interesting and typical accounts presentation. Out of interest the audited accounts which comprised 19 pages were part of an annual report of 55 pages. The remainder of this chapter is a walk through the Rank accounts and the relevant page references are included.

The report of the auditors (page 79)
To understand the significance of this report it is first necessary to put it into some perspective. It is the responsibility of the directors to produce the set of accounts and then for the auditors to report on them. In practice especially in the case of smaller companies the auditors may assist in the selection of appropriate accounting treatments and presentation, but this should not be allowed to cloud the fundamental responsibilities.

In this example, the audit report has been presented at the front of the accounts. It appears sometimes on the same page as the balance sheet or at the very end of the accounts section. Audit reports have almost standard wording and usually consist of two sentences or paragraphs. The first states what the auditor has done (the scope paragraph) and the second gives the auditors opinion (the opinion paragraph). If the auditor has any reservations in his opinion this will be expressed by another paragraph between the scope and the opinion explaining this reservation.

Notice that this audit report contains a second opinion paragraph being the opinion on the current cost accounts supplement. This feature of the audit report will become increasingly common while the annual reports contain separate statements produced under the current cost convention.

Note that the auditor states only his 'opinion' in the report, and does not actually certify the accounts. The proportion of transactions that any auditor can examine and assets and liabilities which can be verified is not large for a company such as Rank, where the volume of transactions is immense. The auditor must assess the strengths and weaknesses of the company's own system and controls, select samples using his professional judgement and form opinions on these. Errors can still go undetected because clearly the auditor cannot look at everything. It is up to the auditor to use good techniques to minimise the possibility of material error going undetected and to form an opinion on the basis of what he has examined.

Finally, note that the report states compliance with the Companies Acts. If the report contains nothing to the contrary you can assume also that there has been compliance with all SSAP's issued by the accounting bodies. Unlike the Companies Acts' requirements, these are not legally binding but where they are not followed the auditor must say so. The requirement to produce accounts which are true and fair over-rides the requirement to follow these standards. Therefore where anomalies arise or in the rare cases when the Standard produces an unrealistic outcome, a fair approach should be used. This divergence from the Standard must be disclosed and explained in the accounts and/or audit report.

Group profit and loss account (page 80)
Generally
The profit and loss account is invariably the first page of the accounts themselves, and on a quick read through an immediate observation is how little detail it contains. It seems to be very much the current trend to keep the face of the accounts relatively simple and move the detail into the notes. There is some debate as to whether this is best practice. Although the notes are an integral part of the accounts there is little doubt that an item expressed on the face of the accounts has more impact for a reader than one that is buried in the notes, particularly when the volume of notes is high. (The Rank accounts have 14 pages which is perfectly typical.) Against that it can be argued that where the profit and loss account or balance sheet are full of detail it is hard to see 'wood for the trees'. It is difficult to get the right balance but, ideally, fundamental matters should be dealt with on the face of the accounts.

It is a good habit to get into, when reading accounts and examining the profit and loss and balance sheets to read the notes as

17

and when reference is made to them on the face of the profit and loss account and balance sheets. This helps in relating the notes with the main financial statements to get the full picture and does not leave the daunting prospect of reading through many pages at one go. The remainder of this section walks through the layout of this profit and loss account.

Trading profit
Having stated at the top what group turnover (sales) is, the profit and loss account starts with the trading profit. This might come as a surprise to those unfamiliar with corporate accounts who would perhaps expect this to feature as the 'bottom line'. It really serves to illustrate just what little detail of their trading results a UK Company is required to disclose under the current law. Certain specific items which have gone into producing that figure are required to be disclosed and these are principally in note 2 (page 84).

A few lines further down the profit and loss account is the interest charge. Rank have taken the view that this should be shown separately from the trading profit as it is not a trading item. This is not uncommon but equally it is sometimes included in trading profit, in which case it would have to be disclosed in the note. Whichever way it is shown the Companies Acts do require certain analysis of interest paid which in this case is shown in note 4.

Profit from associated companies
After trading profit of the group companies, this profit and loss account adds the profit from associated companies.

A company is an associate where the investment held is less than 50 per cent of the ordinary share capital (therefore it cannot be a group company) but the investment gives the company 'significant influence' over the other. Until recently the standard of significant influence was greater than 20 per cent of the ordinary share capital. The rules have now become more flexible so that the 20 per cent criterion is no longer hard and fast but it will still act as the point where there will be presumption, albeit rebuttable by circumstances.

18

The area of associated companies is examined in more depth later in the text but, suffice it to say at this stage, where associated companies exist the share of profits proportional to the holding in the associated company is added into the profit and loss account as has been done here with Rank. This is not the same as the consolidation for subsidiaries explained on page 15. There are two important differences.

a. The profits and losses of the holding company and all subsidiaries are fully consolidated to make a group trading profit which is £37.2 million for Rank. Profits or losses from associates however are always shown separately in the profit and loss account. The proportionate share of the relevant associate's amounts is then included in the headings 'Taxation' and 'Extraordinary Items' in the Rank Group profit and loss account. Notes 5 (page 85) and 6 (page 86) respectively show these associate's amounts being included.

b. Unlike the consolidated accounts there is no inclusion in the balance sheet of the share of assets and liabilities of an associate company. The other side of the double entry bookkeeping, to balance the addition of the share of the associate companies' profits each year, is basically an equal addition to the value of the investment held in the associated companies in the balance sheet. This can be seen by looking at note 14 (page 91), under Associated Companies. This is the item 'Share of retained profit and reserves' which is being added to the costs of the shares.

Minority interests

Having now reached the profit before taxation in the Rank Group profit and loss account, taxation is then deducted and the next line is minority interests.

Minority interests represent the amount of the group's trading profits which are attributable to shareholders of subsidiaries who are outside the group.

Return for a moment to the simple example on page 15, that is a holding company which owns 60 per cent of the shares in a sub-

19

sidiary. Basically the profit after taxation will (after adjustment for certain inter company dealings) be equal to the profit after taxation of the holding company plus that of the subsidiary company. However, these profits do not all accrue to the group as holders of 40 per cent of the subsidiary company's shares i.e. the minority have an interest representing 40 per cent of the subsidiary company's profits after taxation. This is taken out of the group profit and loss account as one figure termed 'minority interest', which leaves the profit before extraordinary items.

Extraordinary items

Extraordinary items, the implications of which are looked at in more detail later, are profits or losses which arise outside the normal trading activities of the business. For example if a company whose business activity is to buy and sell food products decides to sell one of its warehouses which is found to be surplus to its requirements, this may be sold at a large profit. Whilst this profit must be reflected in the profit and loss account, it would be very misleading to include this in trading profit. To do so could hide the fact that the company may actually have made significant losses on its normal food product business, and it is this business, not the sale of warehouses, which indicates the trend of trading performance of the company. In this case therefore, the profit on the warehouse would be an extraordinary item. Look at note 6 (page 86) in the Rank accounts which shows various typical extraordinary items. Note all of these arise in such a way that they are not profits or losses arising from the ordinary business activities which Rank Organisation is set up to provide.

As will be seen later there is a great temptation in areas of doubt for a company to try to deem unusual profits as resulting from normal trading but unusual losses to be extraordinary.

Dividends

The remaining items on the profit and loss account are fairly self-explanatory. The total profit attributable to the Rank Organisation Limited of £37.0 million is analysed in note 7 (page 86) as to how much of this was produced by the holding company itself, how much is retained in subsidiary companies and how much is

20

retained in associated companies. From this amount is deducted the dividends to give the final profit retained for the year, which is reanalysed in note 9 (page 87).

Earnings per share

Finally, at the foot of the profit and loss account, is shown the earnings per ordinary share which must be disclosed for all listed companies. The basis for calculation of this is shown in note 10 (page 87) to the accounts. Notice that dividends to preference shareholders are deducted before calculation of earnings for ordinary shareholders. This is logical as preference dividends represent a prior claim before any distribution can be made to the ordinary shareholders. The significance of the earnings per share calculation is further considered later in the text.

Balance sheets (page 81)

Generally

Notice that two balance sheets are presented side by side, being the balance sheet for the whole group and the balance sheet for the company itself. It is a statutory requirement that both of these balance sheets are produced. This is usually in the columnar format used here by Rank but in some cases you may find the balance sheets on separate pages. Note that there is no such statutory requirement to produce two profit and loss accounts, provided certain analysis between the company's own profit and that of subsidiary and associated companies is included in the notes. In the case of Rank this analysis is given in notes 7 (page 86) and 9 (page 87). Notice the structure of the balance sheet. In the first half of the balance sheet are shown the assets of the company which are equalled by the other half of the balance sheet showing how these assets are financed. At this stage it is worth running through the balance sheet and to look in turn at what the various headings comprise.

Fixed assets

These are assets purchased by the company not for trading in the normal course of business but to be kept and used. This will include typically all business premises, furniture and fittings, plant and machinery, lorries and company cars.

In the case of Rank, also included in fixed assets are 'investment properties'. These are properties being held for the purpose of receiving rentals, as opposed to property purchased for use in the business or with the intention of resale at a profit.

The trading of Rank is not the buying and selling of properties, which is why the properties represent fixed assets earning income and why any sale of properties is an extraordinary item - see note 6 (page 86). However, where a company exists to buy and sell properties rather than to hold them for rental income, then this represents the trading activity of the company and the properties would be included in current rather than fixed assets. Extensive detail of the make up of the Rank fixed assets is given in note 11 (page 87).

Interest in subsidiaries

As is explained more fully in note 13 (page 89), this is represented by the actual cost of purchasing the shares in the subsidiary companies and balances due to and from the subsidiary companies Note that this figure appears in the balance sheet of the company but *not* in that of the group. This is because on a group basis the investment in the subsidiary is replaced by the assets and liabilities of the subsidiary in the consolidation process explained on page 15. The amounts due to and from subsidiaries obviously are eliminated by consolidation as there would be equal and opposite amounts from and to the holding company in the subsidiary companies' own balance sheets.

Investments

This is explained in detail in note 14 (page 91). In the case of Rank the shares in the associated companies have been included under this heading although equally these may be shown as a separate item in the balance sheet. The note will always distinguish between listed and unlisted investments. In the case of listed investments the market value, based on the Stock Exchange quoted price, will be shown and extra information relating to unlisted investments will be provided to assist the user in reaching a conclusion as to their value.

Goodwill

This is the value given to a ready made business connection. For example if one were to purchase the business of the storekeeper on the shop corner, the price which he would expect to receive would be much higher than merely the cost of the premises and the stock of goods in the store. He would also build into the price a significant amount to represent the fact the buyer would probably take on many of his regular customers. The cost of getting a business going and developing a market is considerable so that when a ready made business is sold this is obviously reflected in the price. The same thing applies on a much bigger scale on company acquisitions, when the cost of the shares will generally exceed the value of the underlying assets purchased if one is buying into a profitable company. This excess is termed goodwill which is called an intangible asset. Other intangible assets include trade marks and patents. As will be seen later when it comes to interpreting items in balance sheets, these intangible assets have to be viewed very carefully. There is no doubt that they can have considerable value, but when the crunch comes they are just what their name implies—intangible. For example, however much you pay for a patent it really has value only while the product arising has a market. Similarly goodwill has a value only while the business from which it arose is continuing and continuing successfully. Goodwill will be considered in rather more detail later.

Deferred revenue expenditure

This represents amounts which have been spent in the current year but have not been written off against profit in the current year because the income, which it is hoped that this expenditure will produce, will not arise until the next year. Generally, this could be exploration costs, certain research and development costs or perhaps heavy promotional expenditure designed to increase the market share over a period. Whilst this can in certain circumstances be an acceptable accounting treatment, deferred expenditure must be viewed carefully. As is the case with the goodwill, deferred expenditure does not represent an asset in the tangible sense and there is no guarantee that the related future income will actually arise.

Net current assets/(liabilities)

The final item on the assets side of the balance sheet is net current assets/(liabilities). This is found by subtracting the current liabilities of the company from the current assets and is usually the one case where any liabilities are shown (as a deduction) on the 'assets' side of the balance sheet. The grouping of current assets and current liabilities does assist the reader in establishing the liquidity of the company as will be seen later in the handbook.

In the case of Rank the split between current assets and current liabilities has been taken off of the face of the accounts to note 18. This is quite a common practice although it might be argued that the totals for current assets and current liabilities should be shown on the face of the accounts themselves. As mentioned earlier there is no definite answer with regard to whether items are shown on the face of the accounts or the notes.

Turn to note 18 (page 95) to see what items are included under this heading. Current assets are assets which in the normal course of business are expected to be converted into cash at the bank, or cash equivalent, within a year of the date of the accounts. The principal current assets other than cash itself are stock and debtors. The different current liabilities shown in note 18 are liabilities which could be required to be repaid in the next year from the date of the accounts.

Although this will be discussed at a later stage, it is immediately obvious that a company should generally seek to keep current assets in excess of current liabilities. It is no good a company keeping too many of its assets in a form which is not regularly converting into cash when bills are falling due to be paid day by day.

Financing

The other half of the balance sheet shows how those assets owned by the company have been financed. Generally all assets are financed in one of three ways:

a.   By capital put into the company by the shareholders.

b.   By retaining some of the profits made within the company, rather than distributing them to the shareholders.

c.   From loans by third parties.

Share capital
Share capital is supported in detail by note 15 (page 93). There are two sorts of share capital in this balance sheet, *Ordinary share capital* and *Preference share capital.* Preference shares are shares issued with a fixed return. As shown in note 15, these particular shares in Rank are cumulative which means that, should there be in any particular year insufficient profits to pay any dividends the amount is carried forward and paid as soon as the company is in a position to do so.

This is very important for the ordinary (or equity) shareholders because, as the name of the shares suggests, the preference shares get first claim to any profits available for dividend. On the other hand there is a stated return for preference shares and however good the profits of the company are, the preference shareholders will never get more than this. Some preference shares (although not those of Rank) are what is termed redeemable, which means that the company at a fixed future date will repay the holders the nominal value of their shares. Others are what is termed convertible which means that at a future date they can be converted into ordinary shares.

The ordinary shareholders are eligible to receive all of the profits of the company, once the preference dividend has been paid. In fact however, a company would generally only pay out part of its profits by way of dividend to the shareholders and retain a substantial amount within the company to finance the assets which the company requires.

In the case of Rank there is only one class of ordinary shares but such shares can be issued in different classes each with varying voting rights.

Reserves

The next item on this balance sheet (and in this case, the largest) is reserves. Perhaps the choice of title which this item always has in the balance sheet is unfortunate, as it is a popular misconception that this means that this is an amount that the company has kept 'in reserve'—kept in reserve for a rainy day perhaps? As can be clearly seen from this balance sheet the fact that Rank has reserves of £462 million does not mean that it has this amount of cash set aside in the bank, under the bed or anywhere else for that matter. In fact, as note 18 (page 95) shows, the cash holdings are small. In the case of Rank there are three reserves as shown by note 15 (page 93). The first is a *share premium account* which represents the amount paid to the company by shareholders for their shares over and above the nominal value of the shares. This is really a rather outdated accounting convention because, as you only need to look at the financial pages of newspapers to see, share prices change all the time and a £1 ordinary share will rarely cost exactly £1, even on issue, which makes the nominal value relatively meaningless.

Therefore in terms of understanding the structure of a set of accounts, it is better to consider the ordinary share capital and the share premium account together as being the total amount received by the company from issue of shares. The share premium cannot be distributed by way of dividend to shareholders.

Look next at the final category of reserves shown by Rank, i.e. '*Other Reserves*'. One can be grateful to Rank for the simplicity of their presentation. Many other sets of accounts contain numerous different reserves. Common names are Revenue reserve, General reserve, Exchange Equalisation reserve, Asset Renewals reserve, Dividend Equalisation reserve and of course the Profit and Loss Account.

There are two important points to make. Firstly despite all these different names all these reserves arise as a result of some form of profits (less losses) made by the company. These may or may not arise from normal trading activities. They may be unrealised, as in the case of revaluation of assets. But they are some form of profit nevertheless and basically they are profits which have not, and in some cases legally cannot, be distributed to the shareholders.

26

These amounts are therefore only 'in reserve' in the sense that they were not distributed to shareholders. This does not mean however that there are equal amounts of cash being kept in store in the company as the cash from undistributed profits is reinvested within the business in new assets or reduction of liabilities.

The second important point is that although there is nothing legally to stop a company from breaking down reserves under as many different headings as it wishes, generally a company cannot make transfers to and from the various reserves except via the profit and loss account. The only exception to this is where surpluses arise on the revaluation of fixed assets, this forms the other heading 'investment property revaluation reserve' in note 15 (page 93). In this instance the company can increase the value of the fixed assets and make the corresponding entry in a revaluation reserve without the need to reflect this going into and then out of the profit and loss account. It can be seen that the surplus on revaluation of investment properties of £34,597 in note 15 appears also in note 11 (page 87) explaining the movement on fixed assets.

Notice that ordinary share capital and reserves are subtotalled on the face of the balance sheet to give ordinary shareholders funds being the total assets (at balance sheet valuation) that would be attributable to the shareholders after meeting all liabilities.

Minority interests

As explained earlier, in the case of the balance sheet, minority interests represents the share of the assets less liabilities of the subsidiary companies included in the group accounts attributed to the holders of the shares, which are not owned by the holding company.

Deferred taxation

This is supported in detail by note 17 (page 95). Deferred taxation arises because the rules by which the Inland Revenue determine the profit on which a company pays tax are not the same as those used by accountants to draw up a set of accounts. The deferred taxation account is a technique used by accountants to try to eliminate distortions that this might cause and spread the total amounts of taxation assessed by the Inland Revenue in a way that is more consistent with the accounting policies used in preparing the accounts. Therefore, it in no way changes the tax that you actually pay, just the timing of when this is reflected in the profit and loss account. There are three principal areas and the deferred taxation balance is analysed in note 17 (page 95) into three headings ie capital allowances, stock appreciation relief, and other timing differences—each of which is now considered separately.

a. *Capital allowances* are merely a standard form of depreciation which are used by the Inland Revenue. For accounts purposes companies use a wide variety of depreciation rates and clearly it would not be acceptable to the Inland Revenue for companies to select their own different bases as the choice would effect the amount of tax they pay. Therefore to determine the profit which is assessed for tax, the depreciation used in the accounts is added back and the capital allowances used in its place. The problem can best be seen in the case of plant and machinery where the Inland Revenue normally allow 100 per cent depreciation in the first year. However, in the accounts the asset may be written off at say 10 per cent per annum. The effect in the accounts would be that although profits before tax for the ten years would be equally affected by the depreciation charge each year, profits after tax would be much higher in the first year (because of the big capital allowance received) and correspondingly lower for the next 9 years. In order to make the tax treatment match the accounting treatment the deferred taxation account is used as a sort of suspense account and the effect of the big initial capital allowance is spread evenly over the ten years.

b. *Stock appreciation relief.* This relief was granted by the government to offset the effect of inflation on a company's tax burden. For example if a company held at the beginning of the year 100 items which each cost £3 it would show opening stock of £300. Suppose at the end of the year it also held 100 items but, because of inflation, these new items cost £3.50 each, then there would be a closing stock of £350. Therefore even though the level of stock holding had not changed i.e. 100 items, this would contribute £50 to profit and tax would have to be paid on this. The government recognised that it was unfair to tax this inflation element of profit and therefore granted relief in the above example of £50 (less a few special adjustments) against the profits assessed for tax. As the Inland Revenue could have clawed back relief if stocks fell, deferred taxation was set up to the extent that it seemed probable that relief could be clawed back. The Finance Act 1981 now grants stock relief by an index applied to the opening stock which estimates the inflation rate for stock. Claw back will generally not now apply unless trade substantially ceases. These new rules mean deferred tax on stock relief will become rare.

c. Other differences. These generally occur because accounts are prepared on an accruals basis but certain items are dealt with for tax purposes on a cash basis. Take another simple example and assume that a company pays loan interest of £25 per quarter. Assume also that the company settles the first three due instalments during the year but settles the last one after the year end. An accruals basis used for the accounts means that interest paid for the year will be shown as £100 being total payments relating to the year with a £25 creditor set up, but for the taxation treatment of interest, only items actually paid are allowed. Thus £75 would be the allowable charge and again taxation would not move in relation to profits in the accounts. Assuming next year payments were made on time the interest charge in the accounts would again be £100 but the amount allowed for tax would be £125. Of course in total over the two years the answer is the same, it is purely a question of different timing arising from the two methods. As for capital allowances the deferred taxation account is used as a suspense account to smooth out the effect.

Until 1978 when a statement of accounting practice (SSAP 15) on the subject was issued, the general policy of most companies was to provide for all taxation deferred as well as what was actually assessed. This was provided however unlikely that a liability would arise. This was pertinent in relation to stock appreciation relief where although relief could be reclaimed if the value of stock fell in a year, in practice, due to inflation, the value almost always rose. Although a fall in value could happen, there is certainly a base level for most companies below which it is inconceivable the value could fall unless the company was to cease to trade. Therefore it was obvious that the deferred taxation which related to this portion was never going to be paid. Equally with regard to capital allowances, because companies are continually buying new assets, there is an element of the deferral which is permanent unless the company were to wind down and sell off all its fixed assets. As a result most companies now use the method adopted by Rank (see note 1(x)) (page 84) which is to set up deferred taxation only 'where it cannot be demonstrated with reasonable probability that tax reliefs obtained will continue to benefit the Group for the foreseeable future'.

Loan capital and borrowed money
This is analysed in note 16 (page 94). This shows much detail about the terms on which this money was borrowed, the extent to which these amounts are secured and the dates when they are repayable. Note that the amounts repayable within one year are included in current liabilities.

Source and Application of Funds (page 82)
Generally
Having now worked through the company's balance sheet, the next page is the source and application of funds statement. How is this statement prepared and what does it purport to show?

Entries in the books of a company which go to make up a set of accounts really come from three basic sources

a. Items actually paid for in cash or items which cause cash to be received

b. Items for which the company has not settled cash, but for which a credit exists or conversely items where a debtor exists and cash will be received in future.

c. Items not involving the movement of funds.

Items not involving the movement of funds
These are entries in the books which do not result from buying and selling or extending and receiving credit but are made by the

company's accountant at the year end in order that the accounts correctly reflect the current position. For example whether a company decides that depreciation should be provided to write the asset off over 5 years, 10 years or 20 years, does not actually cost the company anything. It is purely an accounting technique which attempts to write off the cost of the asset over its useful life.

Because this writing down of assets is somewhat arbitrary, the profit or loss resulting on sales of assets during the course of their life is equally so. Similarly the declaring, as opposed to paying, of a dividend does not actually cause a movement of the company's funds, nor does setting aside deferred taxation, nor does adding on the share of profit retained in associated companies. They are purely entries made at the year end by the company.

The source and application of funds statement basically seeks to eliminate most of these entries thus showing a summary of the way the company received funds in the year and how these were applied. It therefore consists broadly of the difference between the opening balance sheet position and the closing balance sheet position with re-adjustment where the movement of any assets or liabilities was caused by items not involving the movement of funds.

Items in a funds statement
Look carefully at the different sources of funds in the Rank accounts. The principle source arises from trading profits after deduction of interest paid and adjustment for accounting entries such as depreciation which are included in the trading profit but do not result in a movement of funds. Extraordinary items are losses in the accounts and reduce the funds produced by trading. However, funds are increased by the receipt of dividends from associated companies. The other ways in which Rank received funds are from the proceeds from selling assets, by increasing certain of its borrowings and by issuing shares.

As the statement goes on to show, these funds are used for the purchase of shares in subsidiary companies and other invest-

31

ments, buying new fixed assets, repaying certain borrowings and paying dividends.

The difference between total sources and total applications gives a decrease in the company's working capital of £21.2 million which is then analysed at the foot of the statement into its constituent parts. Working capital is explained more fully later.

The source and application of funds is a restatement of information, most of which can already be found in the balance sheet and the profit and loss account. However, it is reorganised in such a way as to highlight the ways the company has used its financial resources in the year and how these resources were obtained.

As such it can be a valuable tool to explain for example why a company making good profits can still get into financial difficulties.

Notes to the Accounts (pages 83 to 95)
Generally
The notes to the accounts, in the case of Rank, cover 14 pages. As stated earlier it is very much recommended that these should be read in conjunction with the relevant items to which they relate in the profit and loss account and balance sheet. If this approach is followed, most of the notes will already have been read. In fact in the Rank accounts out of 21 notes only 5 (numbers 1, 12, 19, 20 and 21) have not been directly referenced to the profit and loss account or balance sheet and it is worth some brief commentary on these.

Accounting policies
Note 1 sets out the accounting policies used by the company in the preparation of the accounts. This is almost always the first note to any set of accounts or is sometimes presented separately before the accounts. In terms of its content, for many sets of accounts, it is informative but nevertheless disappointing in the degree of help it gives to the user. The note does give the different policies used in most accounting areas, which does help a user to understand the accounts and see the extent to which the policies used make

any particular set of accounts comparable with those of another company. Frequently however, the notes are found not to explain quite as much as may at first seem to be the case. For example, it is common to see a policy stated that stock is valued at the lower of cost and net realisable value, when in fact there are several different bases for establishing cost which can give different results. It is for the company to select that which in the circumstances gives the fairest reflection of its activities.

Also when one gets into accounting topics, such as leases, foreign currency, goodwill and pensions, the accounting treatment is fairly complex and it is difficult to explain succinctly in a note of acceptable length exactly how the figures are produced. The wording does therefore tend to become rather standardised. Two companies, which appear from the broad comments in the accounting policy note to be comparable, may in fact deal with the topics in rather different ways. Nevertheless, this is important information which should be read carefully and the broad policies which are adopted by the company noted.

Capital expenditure
Note 12 (page 89) deals with future capital expenditure of the company. This disclosure is a statutory requirement and does give a useful indication of future investment plans. This is always split in the way which it is presented in the Rank accounts; the commitments being amounts which the company has actually contracted for, and the further amounts which the board has given authorisation to purchase but which have not been contracted for prior to the year end.

Contingent liabilities
Contingent liabilities, set out in note 19 (page 96), are liabilities which could well crystallise in the future but at present appear only in the notes to the accounts. These typically cover legal claims, guarantees and various taxation matters which have not been finalised with the Inland Revenue.

There is obviously a temptation for any company to show liabilities as contingent because this requires only a note to the accounts. Once the company decides to recognise the liability in the balance sheet itself a provision is required thus reducing profits. Where there is a legal claim against which the company really feels that it has a good defence, this is a genuine contingency. Where however a company knows it will face significant damages and the only unknown is how much they will be, it could be that there is a certain level of liability which is beyond dispute and this amount is not really a contingency at all, and should be provided.

Although in these circumstances it would be the responsibility of the auditor to express reservations in the auditor's report where omission is material, there is no doubt that in practice this is a grey area. Being a grey area unfortunately the note may not give the reader the information to form an accurate opinion of whether the liability will actually arise. There are therefore no rules for the user, except to read the details and nature of these contingent liabilities carefully.

Notes 20 and 21 (page 96) fulfil statutory requirements to disclose details of remuneration paid to directors and certain employees.

The Implications of some
Difficult Areas

Generally

The first chapter concluded by suggesting that accountancy is not an exact science. Perhaps this statement should be put into some perspective. Probably 99 per cent of the entries recorded in a company's books involve recording transactions dealing with the movement of cash (or granting of credit). Broadly one can say that for these entries accounting is an exact science and the process of summarising those resulting figures from the books into the year end accounts is a precise exercise.

The remaining 1 per cent consists of the accounting entries which do not involve the movement of funds as explained earlier.

These entries do not result from the flow of funds and are made at the year end by the accountant to assist in producing a true and fair view of the company's position. But, as soon as entries are not directly related to fund movements, there becomes a element of judgement by the accountant as to which accounting entries will most accurately reflect the current position.

These entries may make up a very small proportion of the total entries made in the books in the year, but their effect can be considerable.

This section of the Handbook will look at some areas where these accounting entries are most significant. These topics represent complex accounting areas so inevitably they can only be looked at to a degree to enable users of accounts, who are non-accountants, to get a understanding of how these figures arise and some points to watch for.

Associated Companies
The basic principles for the treatment of associated companies were dealt with earlier in the text. As stated this treatment can arise for investments in which the company has a holding ranging from 20 to 50 per cent, in certain circumstances it can even apply to less than 20 per cent. The reader should be careful to understand the implications of this accounting treatment. Remember that, under this treatment, the appropriate proportion of the associated company's profit or loss for the year is brought into the investing company's profit and loss account and an equal amount is added (or deducted where it is a loss) to the 'investment in associated company' in the balance sheet.

The effect of this in the balance sheet is to write up the investment, but the resultant figure does not necessarily bear any relation to its market value. Further, it is essential to realise when looking at the profit and loss account that the item 'profit from associate companies' does not actually constitute any flow of cash into the company at all, it is purely an accounting entry.

The only funds that actually flow up from an associated company are dividends which may of course be significantly less than the share of profits. Although a holding of less than 50 per cent can still represent significant influence, it is not an overall majority and therefore the company cannot necessarily control the dividend policy. The purpose here is not to question whether it is correct to include the results of associated companies in this manner. It has been a subject of long debate and one on which an SSAP has been issued requiring this treatment and which is currently being reviewed. However two things should be borne in mind.

a. Do not make the mistake of looking straight at the 'profit before taxation' figure and seeing this as the measure of the company's day to day trading. In the case of Rank out of profit

36

before taxation of £111 million the actual amount earned by the Group was only £15 million. The reader must consider the profit from the associate company separately on its merits. It is not producing actual funds for the group (except by way of dividend), it is merely helping to increase the value of the investment. Although the contribution to profit before taxation from the associate companies is very high in the case of Rank, it can be seen in note 3 (page 84) that in this instance nearly all of that profit comes from associated companies which are jointly owned with Xerox corporation, and there clearly is significant influence in this relationship, but consider the next point.

b. Where the user needs to be wary is in the case of holdings which are marginal, i.e. hovering around the 20 per cent mark. Obviously then the significant influence and the control over the profits in the associated company is more arguable. There is a real danger that the treatment can overstate the value of the investment, particularly if the dividend record is not good. Also bear in mind that as 20 per cent is a guideline, not a firm cut off, there is a great temptation for a company which holds about 20 per cent shareholdings in a number of companies to deem those which are profitable to be associates but those making losses not to be. This will obviously give the investing company a misleadingly profitable result, so watch these 'marginal cases' carefully.

Extraordinary and exceptional items

The basic principles of extraordinary items were explained earlier in the text. These are profits or losses which arise outside the company's normal course of trading activities. Several examples of these appear in note 6 (page 86) of the Rank accounts and are fairly clearly outside the normal trading business of Rank. However other cases are not so clear cut; consider the following examples:

a. A very large regular customer goes into liquidation with a result that a trading profit of £30,000 is turned into a loss of £20,000 because of a £50,000 bad debt.

b. A product line which has sold well for many years suddenly and unexpectedly becomes technically superceded and as a result a write off of the stock of that line of £50,000 is needed and, again, an expected profit of £30,000 becomes a loss.

c. The research and development department concentrates its efforts for the year on a specific new product which it is sure will be a winner. £50,000 is spent and it is then found to be totally abortive and the expected profit again becomes a loss.

At first sight these might appear extraordinary items; certainly they are not occurrences which a company would expect to happen normally and due to their size they have completely turned around the company's results. However these are all examples which the relevant SSAP gives as *not* being extraordinary items. The key aspect is that they are all the result of trading activities. Companies normally incur bad debts, stock write downs and research and development costs in the course of business. Just because the particular amount involved in one year happens to be very large does not turn it into an extraordinary and hence non trading item.

Therefore the examples given above would all be included in the profit (or loss) before taxation and not further down the profit and loss account under extraordinary items. They would however require to be disclosed in the accounts as the Companies Acts require disclosure of normal trading items which in any particular year are of exceptional size.

It can be seen that distinction between these 'exceptional' items and 'extraordinary items' is not always clear cut. At first sight this might seem a rather academic point since it all gets included in the profit and loss account in the end, it is just a matter of which position it is shown in. However it does have significance because the whole purpose of isolating extraordinary items is to eliminate them for the purposes of assessing normal trading performance. Thus earnings per share are calculated on profits before extraordinary items (see Rank for example) and when annual reports show profit trends for a number of years again extraordinary items are omitted.

Thus an item classed as 'exceptional' is included in the profit before taxation and hence in earnings per share and profit trends, but this is not the case where it is classified as extraordinary. This is the reason why, when an amount is included as an extraordinary item, you often hear it described as being included 'below the line' as in some respects it is below the line in the profit and loss account which many users take as the measure of performance. It is not hard to see the temptation for companies to try to argue that unusual costs which occur are extraordinary, and therefore only included below the line, but unusual profits or income are not extraordinary and therefore get included 'above the line'. The user needs to watch these closely when assessing performance. As the above examples show, items such as large bad debts (or bad debt write backs) large stock write offs or large research expenditure might be quite properly classed as exceptional, but they may be just as unlikely to recur to such a high value, as an extraordinary item. Therefore when assessing future profitability, it may be desirable to eliminate exceptional, as well as extraordinary, items.

Depreciation

There is not a great deal to say about depreciation except to emphasise again that it is a subjective figure where companies seem always to be ultra prudent. In theory the rate of depreciation reflects the expected life of the asset; in other words an asset expected to have a life of four years, would be depreciated at 25 per cent of original cost per annum. Companies almost invariably depreciate assets faster than they actually wear out and have many assets making a valuable contribution to the business, long after their cost is fully depreciated in the accounts. Of course in historical accounts the amount charged to the profit and loss account each year is not merely an arbitrary rate but, because it is based on original cost, it in no way reflects the value of the asset which is consumed in a years trading, or the annual amount which should be set aside for ultimate replacement of the asset. This is one aspect where, if included, CCA accounts give much more meaningful results. If CCA accounts are not included one can only hazard a guess, based on what little information is given, about the age and remaining life of the assets. Broadly the older the assets are, the greater in real terms is the extent to which depreciation, based on historical costs, understates the amount which should have been charged against profits. What the user should be particularly wary of is instances when companies change their depreciation policies. As already stated depreciation is somewhat arbitrary, but at least the impact of arbitrariness becomes somewhat lessened when it is used consistently over many years. If the depreciation rates are changed you should look at the justification given as to why the new policy, which may be equally arbitrary, is regarded as better. There have been some examples of companies changing depreciation policies to bring the result in the profit and loss account more into line with what was expected.

Stock valuation

There is no doubt that this is the figure in a set of accounts which lends itself most to profit manipulation if a company has it in mind to do such a thing. Earlier in the text some of the inherent problems of interpreting a valuation described as the lower of cost and market value were mentioned. The term cost covers a number of different methods which can produce different results and in many instances market value may not be readily available, especially where the product is specialised or perhaps caters for a seasonal market which does not conveniently coincide with the balance sheet date. Often for old stock the only approach is to estimate a reduction of cost for obsolescence, which immediately introduces a further degree of subjectivity.

It is essential to realise that the figure shown as stock in the accounts is not an attempt to show stock at its current value. It is shown partly at cost, the basis of which is often not defined, and partly at market value which may have only been established by estimate. There is generally no breakdown of how much of the stock is stated by each basis.

An SSAP was issued in 1975 which does to some extent clarify the position but it would certainly be misleading to say that it gives a magic formula for producing a correct answer. This is not a criticism of the SSAP; is it possible to produce a set of rules which apply equally well to valuing the stock of a manufacturer, the stock of a property developer and the stock of a farmer? The valuation of each type of stock has its own problems and the answer reached will always need a degree of interpretation of the

Standard and some subjectivity; as such it is imprecise, even after the benefit of an audit. This is particularly true of work in progress and finished goods and the determination of an appropriate level of overheads to include in the costs. The user of an annual report simply does not have the information to go behind the stock figure and form his own opinions, except on a very broad basis, but should be aware of the inherent problems.

Provisions

A provision is an amount set aside to meet a known liability the exact amount of which is not readily ascertainable. Contrast this with the contingent liabilities explained earlier which were liabilities which it was not even certain would arise eventually, and therefore were recorded merely as a note.

Consider an example where a company's factory may have suffered extensive damage during the year which is not covered by insurance. The estimated cost of reconstruction or repair is a known liability at the balance sheet date, but the actual amount may be very hard to assess. In this case the directors would set up a 'provision' on the basis of initial estimates. Assume that then, during the next year, the repairs are completed but at the next balance sheet date the bill has not yet been paid. This is again a known liability in the accounts but it is no longer a provision, as the exact amount is now known. It is now an ordinary creditor.

In a set of accounts provisions are usually included with, or combined with the figure for creditors as is the case in the Rank accounts.

The Companies Acts require the amount of provisions to be shown separately if material, but in practice this is something that published accounts rarely seem to do.

The main concern over provisions is that they do provide scope for profit manipulation. If profits are particularly high in one year, a company can make all of its estimates for uncertain liabilities on an ultra pessimistic basis, setting aside larger provisions and reducing profits, perhaps to save tax or to keep some profit back for next year when prospects may not be so good. The concept of prudence makes a natural argument to support this. However, another year might produce poorer trading results and the company might decide in order to help maintain profit level to have a less rigorous approach on setting its provisions resulting in some being reduced and written back in the profit and loss account, thus increasing the current year's profits. As provisions are, almost invariably, best estimates they do have a degree of subjectivity. Therefore a substantial part of the liabilities are provisions; this does give some cause for concern.

Furthermore, many provisions are set up for liabilities arising from trading activities and thus, if they are written back to profit, they will be written back above the line so increasing the profit on which earnings per share and general profit trends are calculated. Where such amounts released from provisions are material in relation to trading profits as a whole, these should be eliminated when assessing the company's performance in the year.

Goodwill

A brief explanation of goodwill was given earlier and it was noted that goodwill like any intangible asset only has a value while the business is continuing and continuing successfully. A problem at present in UK accounting is that goodwill is an area where there is really no standard for treatment. The lack of standardisation shows itself in two principal ways, being firstly how the figure of goodwill is calculated in the first place and secondly whether or not this is amortised (written off in annual instalments) in the accounts.

The Institute of Chartered Accountants in England and Wales' annual *Survey of Published Accounts, 1979* revealed the extent of the diversity of goodwill treatment.

| | *Percentage of* |
Goodwill:	*companies*
carried at cost	33
written down or amortised	14
written off immediately on acquisition	27
no policy evident at all	26
	100

The accounting significance of goodwill is, to put it mildly, confusing for persons not familiar with accountancy. As was said earlier, goodwill is the intangible value of an ongoing business. Since published accounts are produced for all companies which are, it is assumed, ongoing businesses, why does it appear as an asset in some companies but not in others? Also when it does appear, it is frequently on the face of it for a completely unrealistic amount. Take the figure in the Rank accounts for example: no one would really suggest that the intangible value of the business connection of an organisation which has been consistently profitable and just produced a profit before extraordinary items of £57 million, is only £46 million. The first important point is that a company can never include in its accounts a value for its own goodwill. This is just a common sense practical accounting approach as it would clearly be ludicrous to have directors put an arbitrary value on their own company's goodwill and include it in their balance sheet as an asset; the boundaries of creative accounting would know no limit. Therefore the goodwill you see in the balance sheet of Rank (or any other company) is not the value of the ongoing business connection of Rank itself, but the value of goodwill of businesses that Rank has acquired i.e. the amount paid by Rank in excess of the net assets which it actually obtained, representing the business connections and organisation which they were getting. Therefore if the user is trying to assess the value of a company from its balance sheet it is better to disregard any figure for goodwill shown there, as it does not purport to reflect the goodwill of the company itself.

The value of the company's own goodwill cannot be determined objectively but will be a function of its own standing in the market and its profitability over a number of years.

43

Leases

Leasing is one of the most complex accounting topics and it is beyond the scope of this handbook to explain the details of the alternative treatments. However one needs at least to be aware of the problems as the selection of treatment can give quite different results. Consider two companies who both have a delivery business using in each case, eight lorries. One company borrows money and buys its assets, and hence shows them as fixed assets in its balance sheet charging annual depreciation. The other holds its assets under leases but always has eight lorries, constantly renewing all leases as they expire. It might show no fixed assets in its balance sheet as it does not legally own the lorries.

Therefore these are companies, ostensibly undertaking the same business, for whom there should be comparable results, and yet the structure of their accounts may look quite different just because they are financing their fixed assets in different ways. When it comes to comparison of return on capital employed the result is quite misleading. For this reason there is a school of thought that in the case of the second company where the leased assets are of an almost 'permanent' nature, the company should show these in the balance sheet as fixed assets which they possess with a liability on the other side of the balance sheet to the leasing company. This is obviously desirable for comparability between the companies in the example and some companies are already doing this.

Leasing commitments are always disclosed in the notes so that a user can always form an opinion as to whether the company is involved in widespread leasing activities. The accounting policy note should then be read carefully to show how these are being treated in the accounts.

This is an area where there is no accounting standard and therefore there is a widespread variety of treatments. If a lease is not capitalised then the profit and loss account is charged each year with a rental. If it is capitalised then this is replaced by two charges, one for depreciation and one for interest element of repayments. Over the full life of the lease the total charge is of course the same, as this is purely an accounting technique, and does not actually change the money paid to the leasing company. However in any one year it can make quite a difference to profits depending on which approach is used.

Do not expect the eventual issuing of an accounting standard to necessarily solve all of the problems of comparability. Even if it became a standard to capitalise leased assets in certain instances, there are still a number of ways that the lessee can apportion his expenditure, and the lessor his income, in these circumstances, although probably it would be a requirement to include this in the accounting policy note.

Foreign currency

This is a topic where attempts to set an accounting standard have met with immense practical problems both in this country and in the United States and Canada.

The Institute of Chartered Accountants' *Survey of Published Accounts, 1979* showed that a consensus seems to be emerging for the closing rate method which is broadly the approach described in the accounting policy note 1(iv) in the Rank accounts. However, there was no consensus with regard to the treatment of the resulting profit and loss on exchange which was treated on a roughly equal number of occasions as an item 'above the line', 'below the line', as a movement of reserves, or in many cases a combination of these. As explained earlier, the 'line' in the profit and loss account at which items are included does make a difference to calculations such as earnings per share. Therefore, when comparing companies, it is essential to read the accounting policy notes for foreign currency to ensure that you are comparing like with like. The amounts involved in foreign currency gains and losses can be very material.

Pensions

Perhaps one of the most potentially wide ranging topics in modern accounting is the treatment of pension costs. It is a rather obscure area of accounting where a standard is perhaps long overdue and which, when it does arrive, may bring home the potential enormity of the liability that may arise by way of pensions. The

45

problem is that the liability does not actually crystallise until some way in the future and the massive unknown factor of inflation causes considerable problems in ascertaining its size. For example, most pensions are calculated in relation to a person's closing salary and an employee aged 40, currently earning £8,000 a year, would be earning £265,000 a year at retirement if inflation increases at 15 per cent per year for the next 25 years. The accounting problems are immense. If you set up liabilities on the basis of expected salary on retirement how do you account for the shortfall when perhaps inflation causes estimates to be much more than expected? What happens when the figures change through new actuarial assumptions such as longer expected life?

Other problems can occur when some pension costs are unfunded or where the rights under the pension fund are changed. It is well beyond the scope of this handbook to answer these questions but there are, at present, many possible approaches, not the least common of which is to ignore the problem altogether. There is frequently little disclosure of details in accounts but it is potentially a material hidden liability in company accounts which will hopefully become dealt with more uniformally if and when an accounting standard is issued.

Conclusion
All of these areas described in this chapter are difficult areas where the figures in the accounts are largely produced by accounting entries rather than transactions involving the movement of funds. Because there are alternative treatments, there is scope for creative accounting, not that this need necessarily imply any intention to mislead. There are few hard and fast answers to offer except to be aware of the inherent problems in interpretation of some of the resultant figures in the accounts.

Examination of Accounts

Introduction

Any approach to examining figures within accounts always requires a basis for comparison. The possible standards of comparison against which the current year's figures can be examined are the company's previous results, the results which the company had expected to attain, and the performance of comparable companies.

The second of these, the expected results, would generally mean the availability of the company's budget information. Since this handbook considers published accounts, it is assumed that for most users of accounts this information will not be available. If budgets are available, these are obviously of assistance in assessing performance. There is a possibility that in the future certain budgeted information will become published more frequently by companies, particularly such items as cash flow projections. Comparison to other companies can be useful in certain areas but it must be treated with some caution as one is rarely comparing like with like. As was shown in the previous chapter even for two companies in the same industry there are a variety of accounting treatments in many areas of the accounts which can still affect comparability.

When examining a set of accounts, the user is really looking at three aspects which overlap in many areas:

a. How has the company performed in the year? This can be looked at in trading terms, in the profit and loss account and in terms of utilisation of available funds in the source and application of funds statement.

b. What is the company's current day position? This is principally examined in relation to the balance sheet and, to a lesser extent, using the source and application of funds statement which provides the link between the current and previous balance sheets. Of course the user does not have access to the true current position, as accounts are often not published for many months after the balance sheet date, but this is the best information available.

c. How is the company likely to perform in the future? This requires projecting the past and current results forward into the next year, which obviously requires consideration of the prospects of the company itself, its industry generally and for the economy as a whole. Whether the object is to look at past performance, current financial position or likely future performance, the most relevant standard of comparison available is generally the previous results of the company itself. Where possible these should be viewed over a number of years, to look for emerging trends.

Ratios generally
Another feature of examining accounts is that figures are rarely looked at in isolation but rather in conjunction with other figures in the accounts with which they would be expected to have a direct relationship. For instance a higher volume of sales in the year producing a higher year end debtors balance, due to a greater volume of trade credit being given. This leads to the calculation of various accounting ratios. Accounting textbooks show that a vast number of different ratios can be calculated for any set of accounts. However just producing ratios is a relatively meaningless exercise. One must examine the movement on some of the more important ratios over a number of years and then seek explanation and justification for the resulting movements. One has to be careful not to jump to conclusions as an apparent worsening of a ratio may in fact be the result of a planned management decision and may be compensated by a related improvement in other areas. For example a commonly calculated ratio is to

consider sales as a ratio of debtors. As the volume of sales increases one would expect a corresponding increase in the level of debtors. This is clearly a ratio which on the face of it one would be pleased to see increasing, as this would show that the company is collecting its debts more quickly in relation to the volume of sales and this extra cash is available to earn a return or perhaps reduce an overdraft, and hence interest payable. However one has to ask how this was achieved. If this was by offering large discounts for prompt payment it could be that the effect that this has on profit margins more than wipes out the saving on, for example, reduced overdraft interest.

Therefore ratios can only be looked at as a tool for assisting the user in seeing what has actually happened. The more important aspect is then to see whether movements are reasonable and plausible in relation to the known facts and show trends which will be helpful in assessing the future. A difficulty of course is that published accounts do not disclose full information and in the example above the effect of discounts would not be readily identifiable.

Profit and profitability

It is in the area of profit measurement that the user of a set of published accounts has perhaps the greatest cause for complaint that the information available is somewhat inadequate, to measure both current and future performance.

The only relevant figures disclosed in published accounts are those for turnover and final trading profit. Most companies produce a range of products, sometimes reaching completely different market sectors. Therefore this final trading profit figure is derived from the turnover on all of the different products of the business, with the various margins applied, from which are deducted the overheads of the business. For a relatively simple company with a small product range and uniform margins it is possible, even from the trading profit by looking at a number of years, to produce a rough back of the envelope calculation of the margin being used and the volume of overheads. However most companies have many different products and segments and, because margins on different products within the company can vary so widely and detailed analysis of segments and products is rarely disclosed, these margins simply cannot be worked out from the published accounts themselves. The Companies Act 1981 will result in greater detail relating to gross profit being disclosed in the future.

Therefore this leaves the trading profit as the best available profit measure, but for the above reasons it can provide only a broad view of profit. Trading profit is certainly worth reviewing over a number of years and, although its relationship to turnover cannot be expected to be a constant one due to the existence of fixed overheads, they should nevertheless follow the same trend over time.

To get a measure of profitability as opposed to absolute profit, the result for the year must be related to the resources which the company had available to it in the year to make those profits. Clearly two companies which have each made profits of £3,000 are not equally profitable if one needed £10,000 of finance to produce these profits and the other £100,000. The normal measure is the return on capital employed, given by

$$\frac{\text{Profit}}{\text{Capital employed.}}$$

There are a number of ways of calculating capital employed but the most usual basis is by taking the balance sheet total, which gives the total of all sources of finance except for current liabilities, which are regarded as being inextricably bound with current assets in the management of working capital.

Although averaging may be needed if there is a major injection of investment during the year, generally the opening capital employed i.e. from last year's balance sheet, is taken as the base on which the company earns its current year's profits.

There is also some debate as to what is the appropriate profit figure to use for the calculation of return on capital. The figure of profit used must be consistent with the base chosen for capital employed i.e. the profits before payment of interest or dividend to any providers of the finance of that capital employed. The normal measure of profit for these purposes is therefore profit before taxation and before long term loan interest. Strictly as current liabilities are excluded from the calculation of capital employed, any interest paid on current liabilities or received on current assets should also be eliminated from profit, but this is usually not material.

Thus the Rank return on capital employed is

$$\frac{133,260}{694,225} \times 100 = 19\%$$

This is the profit before taxation £(111,237) adding back interest £(22,033) divided by the 1979 balance sheet total.

Return on capital employed is a measure where comparison with other companies is relevant provided one ensures that the calculations are made on the same basis in each case. Comparisons of return on capital employed to companies within the same industry are particularly relevant in assessing profitability performance, but returns on capital in other industries must also be considered as many companies are involved in a number of different types of business. If the return begins to fall one should look for evidence of the company identifying its most profitable areas and moving its resources into these to maintain or improve the return.

Earnings and dividend measures of performance
The measures of profitability outlined earlier are considerations for assessing the performance of the company and particularly the performance of its management in achieving a good result with the resources available.

An ordinary shareholder in the company has a further more personal motive for examining the accounts with a view to how his investment is likely to be affected by that performance. Obviously the two criteria are compatible, as a well run profitable company must be good for the ordinary shareholder as well. The ordinary shareholder has two principal considerations, the capital value of his investment and his expectation by way of dividends. Different investors value one or other of these two considerations

51

as paramount but in both cases are interested in the total earnings of the company in the year, as this will be a factor which affects the total value of the investment and the year's dividends.

There are three principal ratios which are considered, the earnings per share, the price earnings ratio and the dividend cover.

Earnings per share
This is always disclosed in the case of listed companies and shown usually at the foot of the profit and loss account although sometimes by way of a separate note. Many unlisted companies show this figure as well but if it is not disclosed separately it is not hard to calculate from the accounts; the basis set out in note 10 of the Rank accounts is the most typical approach used.

Obviously the ordinary shareholder wants to see this figure being as high as possible as these represent the residual earnings after payment of interest and preference share dividends. The ordinary shareholder will therefore benefit from these earnings either in the form of it being paid out as a dividend, or by the earnings being retained in the company and reinvested, thus increasing the capital value of the company and hence in most cases the value of his shares. Earnings per share is of course some measure of performance but not in the same way as the return on capital employed. The return on capital employed measures the performance of management in using all the funds available to it, however these were raised. After all in measuring management's overall ability to make a return it makes no difference whether they are given the funds by proceeds from share issues, loans or retained profits.

Earnings per share however looks at management's performance not as this overall skill of making a return on a set amount of given funds, but rather in what they have achieved specifically for the ordinary shareholders. In other words it brings in an extra level of management skill, namely getting the appropriate balance of financing. For example management may have made large overall profits on funds available. However if this was achieved by raising funds by high interest loans or issuing preference shares then, although there may be earnings to pay these lenders, the preference shareholders, the management and employees, there may be little left for ordinary shareholders in the end. Despite a high return on capital employed the ordinary shareholders may still feel displeased with management performance.

Comparison of earnings per share with other companies is not meaningful for shareholders as it does not relate to the value of the share or its original purchase price. A shareholder will be less happy with earnings of 40p per share in a company for which he paid £10 per share than earnings of 40p per share in another company for which he paid £1 per share. For comparability the earnings must be related to the value of the share itself for which the price earnings ratio is required.

Price earnings (P/E) ratio.
This is found by dividing the current market price of a share by the earnings per share. The P/E ratios for listed companies are published daily in the Financial Times. The fact that this ratio relates earnings to the value of shares does mean that comparability to other companies, particularly in the same type of business is relevant. The P/E ratio has long been used as a yardstick by potential investors to seek out companies whose price looks relatively low, for their type of business, in relation to their earnings and hence offer a good value investment.

Of course the price earnings ratio offers no more than a general guide as share prices are affected by numerous things other than the earnings shown by accounts. These include the overall political and economic prospects, availability of finance, prospects in the industry as a whole and prospects in the company itself that these earnings can be maintained or improved.

Dividend cover
This is the measure that an investor would look to who is concerned more perhaps with the likely future flow of dividends than capital appreciation. This is found by dividing the earnings used in calculating earnings per share by the ordinary dividends. Companies generally are reluctant to reduce dividends over those

paid in the previous period, as a fall in the shareholder's return can have an adverse effect on the share price. It is common therefore if profits fall below expectation that the amount retained is reduced and the dividend level maintained if possible, only being cut as a last resort. A dividend which represents a smaller proportion of existing profits is better protected against possible falls in the future.

For Rank the dividend cover is $\frac{56464}{21815} = 2.6$ times

This ratio is perhaps not useful in isolation as a prediction of the likelihood that the dividend will be maintained in the next year. It is better to examine the future earnings potential and the past dividend record of the company over a number of years to see whether the company's policy has been to keep dividends fairly constant, to gradually increase them, or to allow them to fluctuate up and down with earnings.

Measures of the company's liquidity
Being profitable is obviously essential for any company in the long term but it is not enough in itself. Unless the company is converting its credit sales into cash with sufficient regularity it may still get into financial trouble by not meeting all of its debts as they fall due. There is a considerable lag in any business between incurring the costs of raw materials, labour and overheads, in making and marketing a product and the actual receipt of the cash after the sale. This lag has to be financed and this finance is generally termed working capital in contrast to long term capital which is used to finance the fixed assets of the business. The most common sources of working capital are the proceeds of sales which can then be used to purchase more raw materials etc. after taking full advantage of periods of credit offered by the company's suppliers, just as the company's customers will in turn require credit before settlement.

The greater the volume of trade, the greater the number of goods for which this lag has to be financed and hence the greater the working capital requirements. A failure to recognise this leads to what is termed over-trading by which a company rapidly expands its volume of business, often producing good profit figures, but fails because working capital has not been increased sufficiently in that time to ensure there is always enough cash to pay suppliers as and when amounts are due.

The standard text book approach to examining liquidity is by the calculating of two ratios:

$$\text{Current ratio} = \frac{\text{current assets}}{\text{current liabilities}}$$

$$\text{Quick ratio} = \frac{\text{current assets—stock}}{\text{current liabilities}}$$

This is one area of interpretation where the use of ratios, without really looking behind the figures produced, can be particularly misleading.

The current ratio is fairly self explanatory and assumes that current assets are all available at relatively short notice to be applied against current liabilities and that current assets such as stock and debtors broadly convert into cash at the same rate as creditors require to be paid. The quick ratio is a stricter measure of liquidity which assumes stock cannot be turned into cash quickly and therefore should not be included. In truth the reality of the liquidity of stock lies somewhere between the two situations of either entirely including or excluding stock. If a company needs funds quickly, stock can often be converted to cash more rapidly than in the normal course of business but of course to do so will probably adversely affect profits as large discounts and advertising may be needed to achieve this. Also stock must be replaced within a relatively short time if the business is to keep going.

For the Rank accounts these ratios are as follows:

	1980	**1979**
Current ratio	$\dfrac{242257}{213201} = 1.14$	$\dfrac{252238}{197502} = 1.28$
Quick ratio	$\dfrac{242257 - 108979}{213201} = 0.63$	$\dfrac{252238 - 110189}{197502} = 0.72$

It is not possible to set any standards as to what is the 'correct' or ideal ratio for a company to have. It depends entirely on the situation of the industry which it is in, particularly as to what is the normal lag between incurring costs on a product and receiving the revenue, and also on other factors below. One common misconception is that a high current, or quick ratio is automatically good and vice versa. Whilst it is clearly management's responsibility to see the ratio does not fall to a level where the company has problems meeting debts when they fall due, subject to this, it should be the aim of management to keep working capital requirements to a minimum as this is tying up capital which could profitably be invested elsewhere in the business. This can be a significant cost.

Thus management will seek to attain ratios which give a reasonable base of working capital. Rather than judge these ratios against some arbitrary standard it is better to examine them within the company over recent years. If they are reasonably constant then working capital is probably at a level which the company finds workable. However, where there is deterioration there is cause for concern. In the case of Rank the ratios might be judged a little low on first sight and yet they are fairly constant over a period of years; in fact very close to their 1978 levels (not reproduced here). It would appear that this company has found its acceptable working ratio.

Another point to note is that for a company's normal annual transactions, it is really the absolute difference between current assets and current liabilities (net current assets) which represents the 'cushion'. Obviously if a company had current assets of £2,000 and current liabilities of £1,000 in year one and £101,000 and £100,000 in year two it would have become much less liquid even though the net current assets are constant. But on normal fluctuations of business activity one should not be too concerned over a change in the ratio if net current assets are fairly constant. Ratios are more open to manipulation than are net current assets since ratios can be changed at the year end by prompt or delayed payment of creditors, whereas this will make no difference to net current assets as it would change current assets and current liabilities by equal amounts.

There are other factors to be considered in viewing the adequacy of liquidity than just current assets and current liabilities. Firstly what is the likelihood of further finance being available? This is largely a function of the economic climate generally, the company's profitability record, its available security and the extent to which it has already required overdrafts etc. For example there is little doubt that were a company with the standing and record of Rank to misjudge its working capital requirements it would have little difficulty obtaining some short term finance. However a less profitable or less proven company may not have the certainty of this option and so may need to work with a higher current asset ratio. While looking at the availability of finance consider the more medium term liquidity requirements such as loans coming close to repayment dates. Does the company appear to look sufficiently attractive in terms of trading, liquidity and security to expect further loans to be forthcoming, or has it assets which can be sold off to repay the loan without impairing its trading ability? When considering the adequacy of liquidity levels look at the make up of the assets in the balance sheet other than current assets.

Holdings of investments, whilst properly not classed as current assets because the company has no intention of selling them, are much more liquid than fixed assets as they could, if necessary, be sold with less disruption to trading; particularly government stocks or listed investments. They do therefore offer a liquidity safeguard which permits a company to work with lower working capital ratios.

Finally while looking at the other assets and liabilities as a whole one should ensure that the company does indeed have a surplus of total assets over its total liabilities, without which the company is in apparent difficulties. In addition to the fact that the profitability record must have been bad, there may be no security for future lenders and further finance could probably come only from the shareholders themselves. Of course in this instance it is more appropriate to view assets at their current values which may be well in excess of those in the balance sheet. If CCA accounts have been included this will obviously help. In the case of Rank there is a healthy surplus even on the historical figures of £564 million (£718.3 million—£150.6 million—£3.7 million). Where the surplus of assets over liabilities is at all marginal it is desirable to exclude any intangible assets such as goodwill from the calculation.

If working capital ratios show a significant worsening this is generally because the company is maintaining stock at too high a level, not collecting its debts promptly enough or paying its own debts too quickly. These can be examined by further ratios for successive years which will indicate to you which of these offers the likely explanation.

Stock turnover ratio $= \dfrac{\text{Turnover}}{\text{Stock}}$ Generally companies do not wish to see this ratio decreasing unless perhaps management is building stock for a particular sales drive.

Debtor turnover ratio $= \dfrac{\text{Turnover}}{\text{Debtors}}$ Generally companies do not wish to see this ratio decreasing unless perhaps by collecting debts more slowly they have made a correspondingly greater saving in discounts given, or perhaps plan to increase total sales by more extended credit terms being offered.

Creditor turnover ratio $= \dfrac{\text{Purchases}}{\text{Creditors}}$ Generally companies do not wish to see this ratio increasing as quicker payments of creditors means more working capital will be needed, unless this disadvantage is outweighed by a greater cash discount being received for prompt payment. It may not be possible to calculate this ratio as the figure for purchases is not usually disclosed in published accounts.

These three ratios should be used only for the broadest conclusions because, as indicated earlier, movements on these can
represent perfectly sound management decisions on which the
user of published accounts is unlikely to have enough information. However, when looked at over a number of years they do
give the basis of a trend.

Financial structure
Companies raise their long term external finance in two basic
ways; by the issue of shares or by long term loans which may take
the form of debentures.

As explained earlier share capital can take the form of ordinary
shares or preference shares.

Ordinary shareholders are entitled to all of the profits after payment of interest to long term loan lenders and payment of preference dividends. By nature preference shares are more similar to
fixed interest loans than to ordinary shares. They have a fixed
return which, as their name suggests, is paid out before any dividend on ordinary shares. However in two respects they are less
attractive for holders than long term loans. Firstly there is no
guarantee, if profits are low, that they will get any return at all as,
like any other dividends, they are only paid at the recommendation of the directors. (Against this it must be said that preference shares are usually cumulative which means if their fixed
dividend is not paid in a particular year through lack of available
funds, it is accumulated and must be paid in a later year before
any dividends can be paid to the ordinary shareholders.)

Secondly, whereas most long term loans are given only after
security has been provided, preference shares are not secured and,
if the company should go into liquidation, will rank behind all of
the creditors and lenders. For these reasons preference shares are
becoming increasingly less common. In fact in the case of Rank
these represent a relatively small proportion of the finance of the
company.

Due to the similarity in the nature of preference shares to loan
capital, these are usually considered together when considering

this source of finance of the company as against the alternative finance provided by ordinary shares.

From the point of view of an ordinary shareholder, it is generally important that the company balances its financial structure between loan capital and ordinary shareholders' funds, as the loan capital will always get a prior payment from funds generated by operations in the year before the ordinary shareholder. Because the payments on loan capital are fixed this means that the greater the element of finance by loan capital, the proportionately greater the fluctuations in profits available for ordinary shareholders.

Consider a simple example where a trading income of £200,000 was made in year one and £150,000 in year two. Set out below are the resulting profits available for distribution to ordinary shareholders in five companies each making these results and each requiring £1,000,000 of finance but obtaining this finance in different mixes of loans and share capital. Note that taxation is ignored as this would affect all figures in equal proportions.

Com-pany	Capital Structure			Profit (after interest)		Percentage Fall in Profits Available for Ordinary Shareholders
	Share Capital	15% Loan Stock	Loan Interest	Year 1	Year 2	
	£	£	£	£	£	
A	1,000,000	—	—	200,000	150,000	25%
B	800,000	200,000	30,000	170,000	120,000	29%
C	600,000	400,000	60,000	140,000	90,000	36%
D	400,000	600,000	90,000	110,000	60,000	45%
E	200,000	800,000	120,000	80,000	30,000	63%

Note the effect in the final column on the change in profits available for shareholders. In the company which has a large amount of loan capital the fluctuations experienced by the ordinary shareholders can be considerable and there is a greater chance that they could get no dividend at all, e.g. company E if profits dropped by another £30,000.

Companies which obtain a high degree of their finance by loan capital, such as company E, are termed 'highly geared'. To measure this one examines the gearing ratio which is usually measured as:

$$\frac{\text{loan capital}}{\text{loan capital and ordinary shareholder's funds.}}$$

Preference shares are usually included with the loan capital for reasons stated earlier. The ratio in the case of Rank would therefore be calculated as follows for 1980:

$$\frac{150581 + 12598}{150581 + 12598 + 512934} \times 100 = 24\%$$

For 1979 the ratio is calculated as follows:

$$\frac{163819 + 12598}{163819 + 12598 + 468518} \times 100 = 27\%$$

The Rank accounts show a trend of reduction in the level of gearing; in 1978 the gearing was in fact 37 per cent.

As with all ratios there is no 'correct figure'. Much clearly depends on the terms of the loans, which are always given in the accounts and should be read carefully. Obviously if a company has the opportunity to get loans at a favourable rate of interest this will be advantageous for shareholders if the company can make a return on the capital employed greater than the interest rate. If this is the case, the company would be foolish not to take advantage of this even if it did appear from the ratio to become too highly geared.

But as an ordinary shareholder or a potential investor the position must be watched closely if further finance is contemplated or where existing loans are costing more in interest than the return on capital employed that the company is earning, as this is making the ordinary shareholder more vulnerable. Also any note in the accounts that there are arrears of cumulative preference dividends should be noted carefully by a potential investor, as these will have to be met out of future profits before any return to the ordinary shareholder can be considered.

Inflation Accounting

Generally

During the early 1970s there was a marked increase in the level of debate as to the inadequacies of accounts prepared on the historical cost convention due to the increasing rate of inflation. Conceptually there were weaknesses in the historical cost convention long before this period but these become insignificant in comparison to the emerging situation where assets were shown in accounts at values at which they were acquired many years ago, when the costs were currently galloping ahead at around 20 per cent per annum.

Two accounting conventions; *Current Purchasing Power* and *Current Cost Accounting* were widely considered in that time and the development of these accounting conventions started an appraisal of accounting concepts which were equally debatable under the historical cost convention. It was perhaps a little hypocritical that some of these concepts, such as what was really meant by a true measure of profit, the maintenance of capital and the maintenance of operating capacity, should have been used as a basis to challenge the various forms of inflation accounting put forward when most accountants had been happy not to consider their validity at all in relation to historical cost accounts.

Current purchasing power (CPP) accounts

CPP was the first system of inflation accounting presented in exposure draft form in 1973 by the accountancy profession, and it has failed to get widespread recognition.

The concept is fairly simple; the historical accounts are used as a basis and then one index, the retail price index, is used to inflate all transactions, including purchasing of fixed assets and trading, between the date of the original transaction and the accounting date. CPP is a comprehensive system and relatively easy to understand but has not been accepted for a number of reasons.

The system is in a sense neither one thing or the other. In starting with historical data, and updating for retail price movements, it is hard to define exactly what the resulting figures mean. The main criticism is that the use of the single retail price index to adjust all accounting figures fails to cope with the very different ways in which inflation affects different businesses. The retail price index expresses changes in the general purchasing power of money but businesses (other than banks) are concerned with real resources rather than money.

Consider an example of a trader who buys an item of stock for £100 and sells it six months later for £150. If the retail price index in the six months increased by 5 per cent then the profit in CPP terms would be £45 (£150 - £105). The £105 available to the trader to purchase more stock has the same purchasing power as the £100 which he had six months ago. However, consider if the actual cost of replacing the stock now is in fact £108, i.e. the price of this kind of stock has gone up faster than the general rate of inflation. £45 cannot be said to be the true profit on the transaction; although the trader has maintained his purchasing power he is still going to be a further £3 worse off when he actually converts the cash into the real resources which his particular business needs.

The position is equally true for fixed assets which he requires. However in this case not merely can the cost of these assets increase at a different rate to the general level of inflation, but the asset might become superceded by technology and the trader could find that, although he has maintained his purchasing power, when he comes to replace the asset he has no option but to do so with a different asset costing considerably more.

This is therefore the crux of the argument against the use of CPP. There is little doubt that it is more meaningful than historical cost accounts, but adapting these for general inflation does not cure other basic weaknesses of historical cost accounts. The values of assets always change as soon as the historical transaction has taken place but general inflation is only one reason. Technology is obviously another factor, as is the extent to which the costs of fixed assets and stock that each particular business needs to acquire in order to trade, change at a different rate to the general level of inflation. On top of this there are the many factors which make up people's demand for the products that the business is making. After all in the last analysis the value of a fixed asset to a business is not its written down historical cost, or the written down cost adjusted for inflation, it is the future ability of that asset to produce profitably products which can be sold.

As CPP lost favour there was a move towards current cost accounts, but a simplified statement measuring the maintenance of current purchasing power of shareholders funds is still included in supplementary information to annual reports by some companies.

Current cost accounts (CCA) generally

The principles of the CCA system can initially be illustrated using the example of the trader in the previous section. In broad CCA terms the profit made by the trader would be only £42 (£150 – £108) which takes into account the current cost of replacing the actual stock consumed. But CCA goes much further than that. It also values fixed assets at their current replacement cost and calculates depreciation thereon. It deals with the costs which the business effectively suffers in times of inflation by having monetary funds tied up in working capital. Finally, it incorporates the savings in real terms for the company of being able to finance part of the business by long term loans, which are fixed in monetary terms and hence cushion the company against some of the effects of inflation.

The SSAP dealing with CCA, which was issued in March 1980, applies to all listed companies and large unlisted companies which meet various size criteria. It requires the supplements to the historical cost accounts to take the form of a current cost profit and loss account and a current cost balance sheet. It does also offer the alternative of producing CCA accounts as the main accounts, with historical cost information, as the supplement. There is a clear implied hope that gradually the latter situation will become prevalent but this allows everyone to feel their way into the new CCA approach gradually.

The current cost profit and loss account

Reproduced on pages 97 and 98 are the current cost accounts of Rank which follow the format set out in the SSAP. It is interesting to note that the current cost deficit for the year of £26.7 million on page 97 compares to a profit for the year of £14.6 million in the historical cost profit and loss account on page 80.

Looking firstly at the current profit and loss account one sees that the first two lines start with a 'profit before interest and taxation' which comes straight from the historical cost accounts and this is followed by 'current cost operating adjustments'.

This very clearly exposes the working of what is being done

'This is the historic cost profit; this is where it is unreliable; these are the amounts by which it should be adjusted to make it more reliable; and this is the current cost operating profit which you get as a result.'

What CCA operating profit is attempting to achieve is to match against sales a measure of resources consumed in the year in real terms. Since the number of transactions is so high, the calculations in reaching this inevitably include a measure of averaging and indexing, but unlike CPP the indices are not just the general retail price index but indices specifically applicable to the particular aspects of the business.

There are three adjustments which are made to the historical cost operating profit in order to reach the more meaningful CCA operating profit. (See note 2 at the foot of page 97).

Cost of sales adjustment

In its simplest form it can be demonstrated easily using the example of the trader given above.

The historical profit on this one transaction was £50 (£150 – £100). However in current cost terms it was £42 (£150 – £108). In this case an adjustment of £8 would therefore be needed. In reality the calculations are rather more complicated and require the use of average periods of stock holding and indices applicable to each product. However the principle remains the same, which is to charge the profit and loss account with the real cost of the goods consumed in the period. That real cost is the cost to the company of replacing them again. The longer stock is held the greater the adjustment will be, assuming inflation continues.

Monetary working capital adjustment

This adjustment is basically complementary to the cost of sales adjustment and arises where a business buys and sells on credit. If such a business is to be a going-concern, it must maintain not only its physical stock levels, but also its involvement in both buying and receiving trade credit. Suppose that physical stocks represent four months usage, that suppliers are paid regularly one month in arrears, and customers settle their accounts regularly two months in arrears.

Then the resource which the business has to finance is not just 4 months' physical stocks, but also 2 months of trade debtors less 1 month of trade creditors. This additional resource, tied up in credit given less taken, is not consumed in trading transactions and so did not appear in earlier adjustments. However if there is a price increase in the items in which a business trades, then the money which must be committed to this credit resource also increases. Historical cost profits must therefore be adjusted to reflect not only the current cost of stocks consumed, but also the additional amount required to finance trade credit at current price levels.

Some businesses sell only for cash, but themselves receive credit from their suppliers, for example supermarkets. Their net involvement in trade credit is therefore a minus rather than a plus. They do not have to finance a monetary resource, but instead use suppliers' money to finance part or even all, of their physical stocks. In such cases, the net burden of maintaining stocks and of financing their replacement as and when consumed is shared by the trader with his supplier—or even is carried wholly by the suppliers. The monetary working capital adjustment allows for these cases; the adjustment becomes a reduction of the cost of sales adjustment where the business is a net receiver rather than a net giver of trade credit.

Depreciation adjustment

The calculation which was made for the historical accounts is repeated, only this time the current cost of the fixed asset is used which will obviously be higher and hence given a higher depreciation. The adjustment required represents the difference between the depreciation as calculated by the two bases. This therefore increases the depreciation to that required for current costs and hence to some extent charges the profit and loss account with the actual cost of the asset 'consumed' in the period. The proviso 'to some extent' is used because, as a measure of the value of the asset consumed, it is only as accurate as the depreciation policy itself. As indicated earlier companies are not very scientific about matching the number of years over which they depreciate assets with their real expected life. Generally a broad approach is used which usually writes off the asset long before it ceases to have a useful life in the business. With depreciation being so much greater under CCA, and thus hitting profits harder, it might lead to a more precise approach to setting depreciation policy as a whole in terms of relating to the true expected life. The current cost of fixed assets is usually calculated by use of a price index applicable to that category of asset, generally obtained from the UK Government Statistical Service, but sometimes by indices compiled internally by the company based on experience in costs of the company's assets over the years.

Since depreciation changes under CCA, profit or loss on the disposal of fixed assets also must reflect current depreciated costs and the profit and loss account reflects this as seen in note 2 to the Rank CCA accounts.

Having made these three adjustments in the example of the CCA profit and loss account, this gives the current cost operating profit. This is the total profit generated from the use of resources and after allowing for their maintenance at current cost levels.

Loans (interest and gearing)
From this must be deducted the cost of 'loans' and taxation.

'Loans' has the extended meaning of all of the monetary liabilities, less assets, of a business except those which have already entered into the calculation of the monetary working capital adjustment. In most businesses the main items will be long term loans, capital liabilities of leasing contracts, tax and deferred tax liabilities, and overdrafts less cash and bank balances. CCA recognises two types of impact on operating profit as a result of net loans. One is the actual interest payable for the year. It appears in full as the same amount in both the historical cost and the CCA profit and loss account. Interest is the cost of external finance.

The other accounting entry is the gearing adjustment. Gearing was discussed earlier. The gearing adjustment is required conceptually because in so far as the finance is provided by, and is repayable in a fixed amount to external sources such as long term loans and overdrafts, it is those lenders who are in fact financing a part of inflation costs represented by the current cost adjustment. The gearing adjustment might therefore be better worded as the 'benefit from external finance'.

The benefit of external finance, for those businesses which have it, is that the business can account to its shareholders on the assumption that part of the burden of rising prices will be borne by future increased borrowing rather than by the business itself. The borrowings will remain as a proportion of the total resources of the business, so that some of the extra money needed to maintain those resources does not, after all, have to be found out of the shareholders' profit. The gearing fraction is broadly the amount of finance provided externally expressed as a fraction of that amount plus the total shareholders' interest, the share-

68

holders' interest being that in CCA terms. The gearing adjustment is then found by multiplying the three other CCA adjustments by this fraction. It will offset the impact of those adjustments and will be an addition to CCA profits.

Taxation

The charge for taxation in the CCA profit and loss account is the same as in the historic cost accounts. It represents the best estimate of the tax which will actually become payable currently or in the future, as a result of the transactions of the year. The taxation of business profits is technically based on historical cost accounts but has for some years included special adjustments for expenditure on new plant and machinery and for the impact of inflation on trading stock as explained earlier. The effect of this latter adjustment has been rather crudely to give companies some relief for an element of their historical profits which is produced purely by inflation.

The current cost balance sheet

The current cost balance sheet for Rank is shown on page 98.

The balance sheet is to be drawn up in the same philosophy as the profit and loss account beginning from the historical cost figure and substituting the 'value to the business' for historical costs. 'Value to the business' expresses the concept of the amount which it would cost the business to replace that asset at current costs, not the concept of 'What the asset can be sold for at current prices.'

Value to the business is generally measured by current costs, which are normally calculated by applying the appropriate index to historical costs. There are two main exceptions.

   a. Property indices are rather distrusted and therefore the rule for land and building is to find the 'value to the business' by open-market valuations for current use—that is what it would cost the business to replace the asset.

   b. Technological developments in plant and machinery make it appropriate in some cases not to apply any index to the historical cost of plant presently in use, but to base CCA depreciation on a cheaper modern equivalent asset for delivering the same quantum of output.

The modern equivalent asset idea is designed only to improve on the use of an index and is not meant to be a means of adjusting CCA depreciation to the same figure as current or planned expenditure on plant.

The other side of the double entry for all CCA adjustments is a newly created 'Current Cost Reserve' which will appear in the current cost balance sheet and is explained in note 6 to the Rank CCA accounts.

Conclusion

The various areas of interpretation discussed earlier in this handbook such as profit concepts, return on capital employed, earnings per share, price earnings ratio and dividend cover, can all be considered in CCA terms. Measures of profitability and performance, in CCA terms, are far more meaningful than those calculated on the historical cost basis, as the profits and earnings in consideration have been calculated after making the necessary adjustments to ensure that the operating capacity of the company has been maintained.

Measures of liquidity show less contrast as items such as debtors, cash and creditors have the same value in current and historical terms. Stock valued in current terms will however generally have a much higher value than in historical cost accounts.

The change as compared to the historical cost accounts calculations may be quite dramatic. This is particularly so in the case of return on capital employed where the full impact of CCA is felt. This return is basically a measure of the profits earned divided by the amount of assets which were available to earn them.

The effect of calculating this on a CCA basis is twofold and in both cases will cause a significant worsening of the return as compared to that which would have resulted on an historical cost calculation. Firstly the numerator of the fraction, the profits, will in times of rising prices be reduced and secondly the denominator, the assets, will be increased by recalculating these on a current cost basis.

However unpleasant it may be for many companies to face up to the results on a CCA basis, to do otherwise is likely to lead to a diminished operating capability and probably a severe drain on cash resources. Considerable care must be taken in assessing the correct level of distributions against the background of the CCA profit to ensure that those distributions are not in excess of that profit. Any such excess would again reduce the future operating capability of the company.

The balance sheet shows assets and liabilities at amounts which are something close to their value to the business.

The choice of the appropriate indices and decisions on property values or modern equivalent assets means that there is a need for the exercising of a considerable amount of subjective judgement, which has been used as an argument against the CCA approach.

However, this argument is hardly valid. As we have seen in this handbook even historical cost accounts themselves contain many areas of judgement and subjectivity, and this cannot therefore outweigh the advantages of CCA over the historical cost accounts convention.

Other forms of reporting on companies and current developments

The corporate report

The idea of the corporate report began in the early seventies as an attempt to consider the most suitable means of measuring and reporting the economic position and prospects (not solely in financial terms) of undertakings in a manner that was useful to those having reasonable rights to such information.

The essential theme was that accounts had in the past dwelt to a large extent on the interest of shareholder's whereas there is in fact a wider range of user such as potential investors, employees, unions, commentators and the government, who need further differing disclosure requirements and, as such, the traditional accounts should be supplemented by statements which meet the needs of these users.

As a concept the corporate report does not justify much further discussion in this handbook as, rightly or wrongly, it never really got off the ground, and the current government consultative document on *Company Accounting and Disclosure* (Cmnd. 7654, 1979) did not even give it a mention. However, there are two statements, the statement of value added and the employment report that it introduced, which were ideas which have been picked up by some companies in their annual reports.

The value added statement

This statement is entirely optional for inclusion in annual reports
and is in essence no more than a reordering of the profit and loss
account, which can have been prepared either in historical or current cost terms. The process of reordering of the information
stresses the interests of the different groups concerned with corporate affairs and how the wealth created by the company was
distributed between those different parties, who are basically
employees, investors, the government and finally the company
itself in the form of retained profits.

Valued added represents the excess of sales over the direct cost of
materials used and all overhead expenses except those related to
payroll. This value added is then appropriated to employees in the
form of salaries and wages, to investors in the form of interest
and dividends, to the government in the form of taxes or retained
in the company for maintenance and expansion of assets.

These statements are undoubtedly becoming more common and
the 1979 Survey of Published Accounts showed that 84 out of the
300 companies surveyed produced these. The statement is sometimes presented in the form of a pie chart.

As all of the information used in a value added statement, with
the exception of employee costs, is already available within most
sets of accounts, it is hard to see what this statement achieves. It
has been looked at as something of a political statement as it
clearly highlights the amount of value added paid to employees,
which is usually the largest appropriation, and does lend itself to
the calculation of such ratios as value added per employee or
value added per £ of wages paid. These ratios may appeal to either
management or to trade unions depending on what the resulting
figures show. However such conclusions are not entirely reasonable. Value added reflects much more than just the efforts of the
employees; specifically it also reflects the buying skills and the
pricing policy of management.

As the disclosure of wages and salaries information in the profit
and loss account will become required under the Companies Act

1981, the use of the value added statement appears to become more limited.

Employment report
As an extension to the value added report, some companies have gone further than merely to disclose amounts paid to employees and have produced what is termed an employment report. This can give information regarding numbers of employees (required disclosure in all annual reports when the number exceeds 100), analysis of the work force by location, divisional responsibilities, length of service and recruitments. It might include details of days lost, the cost of strikes, employee training, welfare information, and the degree of unionisation. It might further contain certain information in ratio form such as sales per employee, profit per employee, assets per employee or as mentioned earlier value added per employee. Such information can be meaningful for certain readers of annual reports, however at present the disclosure of such employment information is relatively rarely produced and entirely optional.

Companies Act 1981—accounts requirements
The Act in so far as it affects company accounts is in response to the EEC Fourth Directive which imposes certain standards of accounting treatment and presentation on the member EEC countries. The Act means changes in the style and content of financial accounts, the most important of which are summarised below.

This Act requires standardised formats for all accounts. In concept this is a major change for the United Kingdom as there are at present no legally prescribed mandatory formats. In practice however this is not likely to make a great deal of difference for users. Under the Act there are optional formats which are acceptable, and most United Kingdom companies already present their accounts in a format very close to these, subject to some extra disclosure requirements.

Small companies, the definitions of which are set in relation to turnover, balance sheet totals and numbers of employees, are permitted to publish an abridged balance sheet and require no profit and loss account to be produced.

With regard to disclosure and accounting treatment certain extra information must be given in the accounts. The difference between the balance sheet value and the market value of stocks must be shown and more disclosure is required in the profit and loss account particularly concerning gross profit and wages and salaries.

The accounts of the Rank Organisation Limited for the year ending 31 October 1980

This is an example of published accounts and is taken from the Annual Report and Accounts 1980 of The Rank Organisation Limited and is reproduced by their kind permission. The page numbers referred therein are those of the original Report and Accounts.

The Rank Organisation

Accounts

Report of the Auditors
to the Members of The Rank Organisation Limited

We have audited the accounts on pages 26 to 44 in accordance with approved Auditing Standards.

In our opinion the accounts set out on pages 26 to 42, which have been prepared on the basis of the accounting policies set out in note 1 on page 29, give a true and fair view of the state of affairs of the company and of the group at 31st October 1980 and of the profit and source and application of funds of the group for the year to that date and comply with the Companies Acts 1948 to 1980.

In our opinion, the abridged supplementary current cost accounts set out on pages 43 and 44 have been properly prepared in accordance with the accounting policies and methods set out therein to give the information required by Statement of Standard Accounting Practice No. 16.

London
22nd January 1981

PEAT, MARWICK, MITCHELL & CO.
Chartered Accountants

25

Group Profit & Loss Account

for the year ended 31st October 1980

	Note	1980 £000	1979 £000
Turnover		596,723	537,832
Trading profit	2	37,222	43,779
Associated companies	3		
Rank Xerox Companies		89,344	101,889
Others		6,694	5,414
		133,260	151,082
Interest	4	22,023	19,893
Profit before taxation		111,237	131,189
Taxation	5	49,980	53,727
		61,257	77,462
Minority interests		4,210	3,476
Profit before extraordinary items		57,047	73,986
Extraordinary items	6	(20,015)	(323)
Profit attributable to The Rank Organisation Limited	7	37,032	73,663
Dividends	8	22,398	22,330
Profit retained	9	14,634	51,333
Earnings per Ordinary Share	10	28·0p	38·4p

The notes to the accounts are on pages 29 to 42.

26

80

at 31st October 1980

	Note	Group 1980 £000	Group 1979 £000	Company 1980 £000	Company 1979 £000
Assets employed					
Fixed assets	11				
Investment properties		**156,121**	139,426	—	—
Others		**242,450**	223,372	**59,042**	47,408
Interest in subsidiaries	13	—	—	**309,073**	323,005
Investments	14	**243,506**	224,903	**1,202**	4,202
Goodwill		**46,094**	50,774	**3,997**	4,031
Deferred revenue expenditure		**1,072**	1,044	**89**	29
Net current assets (liabilities)	18	**29,056**	54,736	**(35,355)**	(11,430)
		718,299	694,255	**338,048**	367,245
Financed by					
Ordinary share capital	15	**50,498**	50,339	**50,498**	50,339
Reserves	15	**462,436**	418,179	**190,440**	212,436
Ordinary shareholders' funds		**512,934**	468,518	**240,938**	262,775
Preference share capital	15	**12,598**	12,598	**12,598**	12,598
Minority interests		**38,489**	44,103	—	—
Deferred taxation	17	**3,697**	5,217	**2,178**	1,511
Loan capital and borrowed money	16	**150,581**	163,819	**82,334**	90,361
		718,299	694,255	**338,048**	367,245

HARRY SMITH } *Directors*
RUSSELL W. EVANS }

The notes to the accounts are on pages 29 to 42.

27

81

for the year ended 31st October 1980

	1980 £ million	1979 £ million
Source of funds		
Within the Group		
Trading profit	37·2	43·8
Interest	(22·0)	(19·9)
Dividends received from associated companies	23·6	24·7
Extraordinary items before tax	(27·5)	(1·8)
Items included above not requiring (providing) funds		
Depreciation	14·3	12·9
Other items	3·8	(2·1)
	29·4	57·6
Net proceeds from the sale of:		
Investments	4·9	—
Properties and plant	8·2	6·7
	42·5	64·3
Outside the Group		
Borrowings other than bank overdrafts		
Amount repayable within 5 years	15·7	9·3
Amount not repayable within 5 years	8·0	2·7
Issue of Ordinary Shares	1·1	62·4
Issue of shares of subsidiaries to minorities	—	30·4
	24·8	104·8
Total	67·3	169·1
Application of funds		
Acquisition of net assets and goodwill of subsidiaries	3·4	27·5
Other investments	0·3	7·1
Additions to fixed assets		
Investment properties	2·6	2·5
Other fixed assets	37·8	28·4
Repayment of borrowings other than bank overdrafts	16·9	80·4
Dividends paid	25·8	16·8
Taxation paid	1·7	1·7
	88·5	164·4
(Decrease) increase in working capital	(21·2)	4·7
Comprising		
(Increase) in creditors and accrued expenses	(13·4)	(4·1)
(Increase) in acceptance credits and bank overdrafts less cash and short term deposits	(24·2)	(13·1)
Increase in stock and work in progress	2·7	12·2
Increase in debtors	13·7	9·7
	(21·2)	4·7

Note: To eliminate distortions arising from changes in foreign currency exchange rates, the figures are presented on the basis that exchange rates ruling at 31st October of each year had applied throughout that year.

28

1 Accounting policies

(i) Historical cost convention
The accounts of the Group have been prepared under the historical cost convention, adjusted for the revaluation of certain properties as disclosed in note 11.

(ii) Subsidiary companies
The Group accounts include the audited accounts, made up to 31st October 1980, of all subsidiary companies. Details of principal subsidiary companies are given in note 13.

(iii) Associated companies
The Group Profit and Loss Account includes the proportion of the results of associated companies attributable to the shareholdings of The Rank Organisation Limited and its subsidiaries. The principal cases where accounts have been used which are not co-terminous with those of The Rank Organisation Limited, are as follows:

Company	Accounting date
Cathay Organisation Private Limited	31st December 1979
The Greater Union Organisation Pty. Limited	30th June 1980
Kerridge Odeon Corporation Limited	31st March 1980

In the Group Balance Sheet the investments in associated companies are shown at the aggregate of cost (less amounts written off) and the Group's share of post-acquisition retained profits and reserves.

(iv) Exchange rates
The Company and its subsidiaries
Assets and liabilities and profit and loss account items in foreign currencies are translated into sterling at the rates ruling at the balance sheet date. Exchange differences on trading transactions are dealt with in arriving at trading profit. Realised exchange differences on non-trading transactions, to the extent not dealt with in earlier years, are included in the profit and loss account in extraordinary items. All other exchange differences are dealt with in reserves.

Rank Xerox Companies
Foreign currency current assets other than stocks, and all liabilities other than deferred taxation, are translated into sterling at the rates ruling at the balance sheet date. Stocks, fixed assets (including related depreciation) and deferred taxation are translated at the rates ruling at the dates of acquisition or origin. All exchange differences are dealt with in arriving at trading profit.

(v) Turnover
Turnover consists of sales of goods and services, admission receipts, film distribution revenues, royalties, commissions and gross rents receivable from investment properties and proceeds of sale of properties held as trading assets. Turnover of associated companies is not included.

(vi) Goodwill
Goodwill represents the net excess of the cost of shares in subsidiaries over the net tangible assets at dates of acquisition and is stated at cost less amounts written off.

(vii) Stocks
Raw materials, work in progress, finished goods, other stocks and film productions are stated at the lower of cost (including, where appropriate, manufacturing overheads) and net realisable value on bases consistent with the previous year. Work in progress is stated net of progress payments receivable.

(viii) Deferred revenue expenditure
Deferred revenue expenditure comprises:

(a) oil exploration expenditure which is carried forward until a decision can be reached as to whether or not the project to which such expenditure relates has prospects for development on a commercial basis. Provisions are made to reduce expenditure to estimated realisable value.

(b) pre-opening expenses which are written off on a straight line basis over ten years.

29

(ix) Depreciation of fixed assets
The following is a summary of the Group's policy for depreciation of fixed assets.

Properties held for investment
(a) No depreciation has been provided on freehold land and buildings.

(b) No depreciation has been provided on leasehold properties where the leases have more than 50 years to run. Other leasehold properties have been depreciated on a straight line basis over the remaining terms of the leases.

Other properties
(a) No depreciation has been provided on freehold land.

(b) Depreciation is provided on a straight line basis to write off the cost of all freehold buildings over their estimated useful lives which do not exceed 100 years.

(c) Leasehold properties are depreciated over the shorter of their estimated useful lives which do not exceed 100 years and the terms of the leases.

Plant, vehicles and equipment
Depreciation is provided on a straight line basis to write off the cost of the assets over their estimated useful lives mainly at rates between 5% and 25% per annum.

(x) Deferred Taxation
The Company and its subsidiaries
Deferred taxation is only provided where required by local regulations, or where it cannot be demonstrated with reasonable probability that tax reliefs obtained will continue to benefit the Group for the foreseeable future.

No provision is made for taxation payable in the event of the profits of certain overseas subsidiary and associated companies being distributed and on capital gains which might arise from the sale of properties at the values at which they are stated in the Group Balance Sheet.

The amounts of deferred taxation provided and the relevant potential liability are set out in note 17 on page 41.

Rank Xerox Companies
Full provision is made for deferred taxation.

	1980 £000	1979 £000
2 Trading profit		
Trading profit is arrived at after crediting		
Surplus on purchase of debentures and loan stock	705	1,467
And after charging		
Depreciation	14,302	12,883
Auditors' remuneration (Company £125,000, 1979 £111,000)	908	891

3 Associated companies

	Rank Xerox Companies		Others	
	1980 £000	1979 £000	1980 £000	1979 £000
Share of profits less losses before taxation	89,344	101,889	6,694	5,414
Taxation (note 5)	(44,817)	(49,722)	(3,492)	(2,660)
Extraordinary items (note 6)	—	—	612	17
	44,527	52,167	3,814	2,771
Dividends receivable by the Group	(21,402)	(22,919)	(1,713)	(1,229)
Profits less losses for the year retained by associated companies	23,125	29,248	2,101	1,542
Minority interests	(835)	(1,056)	—	—
Amounts retained attributable to shareholders of the company	22,290	28,192	2,101	1,542
Reserves of associated company written out on disposal of investment	—	—	(1,319)	—
Net increase in profits retained in associated companies (note 9)	22,290	28,192	782	1,542

30

4 Interest

	1980 £000	1979 £000
Interest on bank loans and overdrafts	9,963	10,412
Interest on other loans fully repayable within 5 years	2,871	4,131
Interest on other loans not fully repayable within 5 years	8,061	8,701
Discount on acceptance credits	3,565	814
Interest receivable	(2,457)	(4,165)
	22,023	19,893

5 Taxation

	1980 Company and its subsidiaries £000	1980 Associated companies Rank Xerox Companies £000	1980 Associated companies Others £000	1980 Total £000	1979 Company and its subsidiaries £000	1979 Associated companies Rank Xerox Companies £000	1979 Associated companies Others £000	1979 Total £000
United Kingdom corporation tax								
Current tax	(2,112)	15,794	986	14,668	5,339	16,614	709	22,662
Deferred tax	(1,084)	(1,812)	491	(2,405)	(4,241)	(2,587)	(32)	(6,860)
Advance corporation tax	1,676	—	—	1,676	(1,075)	—	—	(1,075)
	(1,520)	13,982	1,477	13,939	23	14,027	677	14,727
Overseas								
Current tax	1,985	24,259	2,070	28,314	763	38,444	2,057	41,264
Deferred tax	1,206	6,576	(55)	7,727	559	(2,749)	(74)	(2,264)
	3,191	30,835	2,015	36,041	1,322	35,695	1,983	39,000
	1,671	44,817	3,492	49,980	1,345	49,722	2,660	53,727

United Kingdom corporation tax is provided at 52% and is stated after crediting double tax relief of £373,000 (1979 £239,000) in respect of income from subsidiaries and £818,000 (1979 £738,000) in respect of dividends from associated companies. The charge for taxation for the Company and its subsidiaries has been reduced in respect of accelerated capital allowances, stock appreciation relief and other timing differences aggregating £8,020,000 (1979 £9,946,000). The charge for taxation for 1979 was also reduced by £3,797,000 for the Company and its subsidiaries and by £3,980,000 for Rank Xerox Companies in respect of permanent stock relief granted by the Finance (No. 2) Act 1979.

31

85

6 Extraordinary items	1980 £000	1979 £000
Profits less losses on disposal of investment properties (1979 includes surplus provision against diminution in value)	1,315	4,240
Profits less losses on disposals of other properties	607	269
Losses on cessation of businesses	(24,850)	(3,310)
Losses and provisions for losses less profits on disposal of investments in subsidiary, associated and other companies	(1,852)	(82)
Goodwill written off	(3,156)	(2,151)
Exchange profits on repayment of overseas currency loans	399	(737)
	(27,537)	(1,771)
Taxation (including relief relating to previous years)	2,989	1,022
	(24,548)	(749)
Share of extraordinary items of associated companies	612	17
	(23,936)	(732)
Attributable to minorities	(3,921)	(409)
	(20,015)	(323)

7 Profit attributable to The Rank Organisation Limited	1980 £000	1979 £000
Dealt with in the accounts of The Rank Organisation Limited	(617)	35,145
Retained in subsidiary companies	14,577	8,784
Retained in associated companies	23,072	29,734
	37,032	73,663

8 Dividends	1980 £000	1979 £000
Preference Shares		
6¼% Cumulative Preference	437	437
8% Second Cumulative Preference	146	146
	583	583
Ordinary Shares		
Interim of 4·8p per share, since paid (1979 interim of 4·8p per share)	9,695	9,665
Final of 6p per share, proposed (1979 final of 6p per share)	12,120	12,082
	21,815	21,747
	22,398	22,330

By virtue of the Finance Acts 1972 and 1976, the dividends payable on the 6¼% Cumulative Preference Shares and 8% Second Cumulative Preference Shares are calculated at the rates of 4·375% and 5·6% per annum respectively.

32

9 Profit retained	1980 £000	1979 £000
The Rank Organisation Limited and subsidiaries	(8,438)	21,599
Associated companies		
Rank Xerox Companies	22,290	28,192
Others	782	1,542
	14,634	51,333

10 Earnings per Ordinary Share

The calculation of earnings per Ordinary Share is based upon profit before extraordinary items of £57,047,000, from which are deducted Preference dividends totalling £583,000, giving earnings of £56,464,000 (1979 £73,403,000), and on the weighted average of Ordinary Shares in issue during the year of 201,835,000 (1979 191,227,000 shares). If full provision had been made for deferred taxation, other than in respect of capital gains, earnings would have been £48,458,000 (1979 £63,569,000) and earnings per share 24·0p (1979 33.2p).

11 Fixed assets

Group	Completed properties		Properties held for and in course of development		
Investment properties	Freehold £000	Leasehold £000	Freehold £000	Leasehold £000	Total £000
Net book amount at 31st October 1979*	80,450	56,079	2,750	147	139,426
Transfers to other fixed assets	(6,250)	—	(18)	—	(6,268)
Exchange adjustments	(8,174)	(3,850)	—	—	(12,024)
Additions at cost	1,069	658	875	—	2,602
Disposals at book amount	(1,238)	(226)	(637)	—	(2,101)
Depreciation for year	—	(111)	—	—	(111)
Surplus on revaluation	16,662	17,415	430	90	34,597
Directors valuation at 31st October 1980	82,519	69,965	3,400	237	156,121

*The opening balances have been adjusted in respect of assets reclassified.

The Group's investment properties have been revalued as at 31st October 1980 by the Directors (with advice from executives of the Group who hold appropriate professional qualifications), on the basis of the value to the Group on an existing use basis.
The net surplus of £34,597,000 arising from the revaluations, including a net surplus on overseas investment properties of £9,375,000 translated at exchange rates ruling at 31st October 1980, has been transferred to an investment property revaluation reserve.

33

87

Fixed assets *continued*	Freehold land and buildings £000	Leasehold land and buildings £000	Plant, vehicles and equipment £000	Total £000
Other fixed assets				
At cost	131,529	64,648	137,263	333,440
At Directors' valuation in				
1973	6,250	—	—	6,250
1975	849	—	—	849
1978	1,039	—	—	1,039
1979	250	—	—	250
	139,917	64,648	137,263	341,828
Accumulated depreciation	26,070	10,149	63,159	99,378
Net book amount at 31st October 1980	113,847	54,499	74,104	242,450
Movements during year:				
Net book amount at 31st October 1979*	108,916	45,679	68,777	223,372
Transfers from investment property	6,268	—	—	6,268
Depreciation for prior years on transfer from investment property	(276)	—	—	(276)
Exchange adjustments	(5,688)	(510)	(2,002)	(8,200)
New subsidiaries	840	83	884	1,807
Additions at cost	6,266	11,283	20,279	37,828
Disposals at book amount	(382)	(772)	(2,497)	(3,651)
Provisions for losses on disposal	(76)	16	(350)	(410)
Depreciation for year	(2021)	(1,280)	(10,987)	(14,288)
Net book amount at 31st October 1980	113,847	54,499	74,104	242,450
Company				
At cost	27,786	25,418	35,519	88,723
Accumulated depreciation	7,354	4,537	17,790	29,681
Net book amount at 31st October 1980	20,432	20,881	17,729	59,042
Movements during year:				
Net book amount at 31st October 1979*	19,691	12,082	15,635	47,408
Inter group transfers at book amount	18	—	(38)	(20)
Additions at cost	1,314	9,278	5,200	15,792
Disposals at book amount	(144)	(102)	(208)	(454)
Provision for losses on disposal	(76)	16	(350)	(410)
Depreciation for year	(371)	(393)	(2,510)	(3,274)
Net book amount at 31st October 1980	20,432	20,881	17,729	59,042

*The opening balances have been adjusted in respect of assets reclassified.

The net book amount of investment properties and other leasehold land and buildings at 31st October 1980 includes for the Group £13,596,000 (1979 £13,243,000) and for the company £6,339,000 (1979 £5,820,000) in respect of leases with less than 50 years to run. The net book amount of investment properties at 31st October 1980 not depreciated during the year ended on that date was, in respect of the Group £152,688,000 (1979 £137,467,000).

34

12 Future capital expenditure

	Group		Company	
	1980	1979	1980	1979
	£000	£000	£000	£000
Commitments	6,006	6,468	648	428
Authorised by the Directors but not contracted	9,852	11,577	1,585	3,422
	15,858	18,045	2,233	3,850
United Kingdom	14,028	14,492		
Overseas	1,830	3,553		
	15,858	18,045		

13 Interest in subsidiaries

	1980	1979
	£000	£000
Shares in subsidiaries at or under cost	142,227	142,473
Amounts owing by subsidiaries including dividends receivable less provisions	246,874	254,847
Interest receivable	—	3,115
	389,101	400,435
Less: Amounts owing to subsidiaries	78,755	76,421
Interest payable	1,273	1,009
	309,073	323,005

Of the amounts owing by subsidiaries £74,500,000 (1979 £74,500,000) has been subordinated to other creditors as an alternative to increasing the share capital of certain subsidiaries.

The principal subsidiaries, whose activities are shown in greater detail in the Review of Operations on pages 11 to 19, are:

	Class of shares owned	Percentage of share capital attributable to the Company		
		Directly owned	Through subsidiaries	Total
Leisure services and hotels				
Odeon (Ireland) Limited	Ordinary	—	100	100
Pinewood Studios Limited	Ordinary	100	—	100
Rank Advertising Films Limited	Ordinary	100	—	100
Rank Film Distributors Limited	Ordinary	100	—	100
Rank Hotels Limited	Ordinary	100	—	100
Rank Leisure Limited	Company limited by guarantee	100	—	100
Rank Marine International Limited	Ordinary	100	—	100
Rank Tuschinski Beheer B.V.	Ordinary	—	100	100
Industrial and consumer products				
English Numbering Machines Limited	Ordinary	100	—	100
Rank Audio Visual Limited	Ordinary	100	—	100
Rank Film Laboratories Limited	Ordinary	100	—	100
Rank Industries America Inc.	Common	—	100	100
Rank Industries Asia Pte. Limited	Ordinary	—	100	100
Rank Industries Australia Pty. Limited	Ordinary	—	100	100
Rank Industries Canada Limited	Common	—	100	100
	Non-Cumulative Participating Preference	—	100	100
Rank Precision Industries Limited (note (c))	Ordinary	30	65	95
Rank Radio International Limited	Ordinary	100	—	100
Rank Toshiba Limited (note (e))	Ordinary	—	70	70

35

Details of principal subsidiary companies *continued*

	Class of shares owned	Percentage of share capital attributable to the Company		
		Directly owned	Through subsidiaries	Total
Holiday Centres				
Butlin's Limited	6% Cumulative Preference	100	—	100
	Ordinary	100	—	100
Leisure Caravan Parks Limited	Ordinary	100	—	100
Property				
Rank City Wall Limited	Ordinary	100	—	100
Rank City Wall Canada Limited	Common	—	100	100
	9% 'C' Cumulative Redeemable Preference	—	100	100
Holding Companies				
A. Kershaw & Sons, Limited	8% 'A' Cumulative Preference	78	—	78
(note (a))	12½% 'B' Non-Cumulative Preference	85	—	85
	Ordinary	82	—	82
Rank Overseas Holdings Limited (note (b))	Ordinary	100	—	100
Rank Precision Industries (Holdings) Limited (notes (a) and (c))	5% Cumulative Preference	57	35	92
	Ordinary	60	33	93
Rank RX Holdings Limited (notes (c) and (d))	Ordinary	50	46	96

(a) A. Kershaw & Sons, Limited holds 43% of the preference and 40% of the ordinary share capital of Rank Precision Industries (Holdings) Limited.
(b) Rank Overseas Holdings Limited owns the Group's investment in Rank Industries Australia Pty. Limited and many other overseas subsidiary and associated companies.
(c) Rank-Precision Industries (Holdings) Limited owns 70% of the share capital of Rank Precision Industries Limited and 50% of the share capital of Rank RX Holdings Limited.
(d) Rank RX Holdings Limited owns directly and indirectly the whole of the Group's interests in the Rank Xerox Companies.
(e) Under an agreement dated 23rd December 1980, Rank Toshiba Limited became a wholly owned subsidiary of the Company.
(f) All companies listed above are incorporated and operate in Great Britain other than:

Odeon (Ireland) – Eire
Rank Industries America – U.S.A.
Rank Industries Asia – Singapore
Rank Industries Australia – Australia

Rank Industries Canada – Canada
Rank City Wall Canada – Canada
Rank Tuschinski Beheer – Holland

36

14 Investments

	1980 £000	1979 £000
Group		
Rank Xerox Companies		
Unlisted		
Shares at par	14,883	14,883
Shares at cost	4,145	4,145
Share of retained profits and reserves	196,586	173,461
	215,614	192,489
Subordinated unsecured loan notes	1,200	1,200
Promissory notes	537	537
	217,351	194,226
Other associated companies		
Unlisted		
Shares at Directors' valuation	639	639
Shares at cost less amounts written off	2,725	3,436
Scrip issue at par	902	902
Share of retained profits and reserves	19,952	20,463
Advances	119	113
	24,337	25,552
Listed		
Shares at cost (Market value £125,000—1979 £117,000)	36	48
	24,373	25,600
Other investments		
Listed shares at cost less amounts written off		
(Market value £16,000—1979 £3,259,000)	37	3,047
Promissory note	1,745	2,030
	1,782	5,077
Total		
Unlisted	243,433	221,808
Listed	73	3,095
	243,506	224,903
Company		
Other associated companies		
Unlisted		
Shares at cost	266	266
Scrip issue at par	902	902
	1,168	1,168
Other investments		
Listed shares at cost (Market value £13,000—1979 £3,236,000)	34	3,034
Total	1,202	4,202

37

Investments *continued*
Details of the principal investments

	Country of incorporation and operation	Class of capital owned	Directly owned	Percentage of share capital attributable to the Company	
				Through subsidiaries	Total
Rank Xerox Companies					
Rank Xerox Limited	Great Britain	'B' Ordinary	—	96·4	96·4
		'D' Ordinary	—	96·4	96·4
Rank Xerox Business Equipment Inc.	U.S.A.	'B' Common	—	96·4	96·4
Rank Xerox Holding B.V.	Holland	'B' Ordinary	—	96·4	96·4
		'C' Ordinary	—	96·4	96·4
Rank Xerox Investments Limited	Bermuda	'B' Ordinary	—	96·4	96·4
Other associated companies					
Film Exhibition					
Cathay Films Distribution Company Limited	Hong Kong	Ordinary	—	24·2	24·2
Cathay Organisation Private Limited	Singapore	Ordinary	—	24·2	24·2
Ceylon Theatres Limited	Sri Lanka	Ordinary	—	28·4	28·4
The Greater Union Organisation Pty. Limited	Australia	Ordinary	—	50·0	50·0
Kerridge Odeon Corporation Limited	New Zealand	Ordinary	—	50·0	50·0
Manufacture					
Bush (Ireland) Limited	Eire	'A' Ordinary	—	30·0	30·0
		'B' Ordinary	—	49·0	49·0
Bush India Limited	India	Ordinary	—	40·0	40·0
Murphy India Limited	India	Ordinary	—	33·4	33·4
Property					
Rank Estates Limited	Great Britain	Ordinary	47·5	—	47·5
Television					
Southern Television Limited	Great Britain	Ordinary	37·6	—	37·6

The business of **Rank Xerox Limited** consists mainly of the manufacture in the United Kingdom of xerographic equipment for high speed document copying and duplicating, the marketing of such equipment through subsidiaries operating in Europe, Asia, Africa and Australasia and the manufacturing and marketing operations of Fuji Xerox Co. Ltd., a company incorporated in Japan, which is 50% owned.
Rank RX Holdings Limited owns all the 'B' and 'D' shares in Rank Xerox Limited and is entitled to approximately 48·8% of the total votes. Xerox Corporation and a subsidiary own all the 'A' and 'C' shares and are entitled to approximately 51·2% of the total votes. 57,475 'E' shares in Rank Xerox Limited are held by the Trustees of the Rank Xerox employee share purchase scheme and carry no votes.

Rank Xerox Business Equipment Inc. is an investment holding company which acquired the Eastern Hemisphere Special Businesses of Xerox Corporation in April 1979. These businesses, which are conducted through wholly owned subsidiaries of Rank Xerox Business Equipment Inc. in the United Kingdom, Belgium, France and West Germany, comprise the manufacture and marketing of office equipment and the publication of books and training programmes. Xerox Corporation is entitled to 51% of the voting rights in Rank Xerox Business Equipment Inc. and Rank RX Overseas Limited (a wholly owned subsidiary of Rank RX Holdings Limited) is entitled to 49%.

Rank Xerox Holding B.V. owns the entire share capital of Rank Xerox Manufacturing (Nederland) B.V. whose manufacturing facilities are employed mainly in the manufacture of xerographic equipment and ancillary supplies. Société Industrielle Rank Xerox S.A., incorporated and operating in France, is also a subsidiary of Rank Xerox Holding B.V. The xerographic equipment and ancillary supplies manufactured by Rank Xerox Manufacturing (Nederland) B.V. and Société Industrielle Rank Xerox S.A. are sold mainly to other Rank Xerox companies.
Voting rights in Rank Xerox Holding B.V. are held as to 51·2% by Xerox Corporation and 48·8% by Rank RX Overseas Limited.

Rank Xerox Investments Limited is an investment holding company and owns 75% of the share capital of Xerox Egypt S.A.E., whose business consists mainly of the marketing of xerographic equipment and ancillary supplies.
Voting rights in Rank Xerox Investments Limited are held as to 51% by Xerox Corporation and 49% by Rank RX Overseas Limited.

Under an agreement with Xerox Corporation made in 1977, the Group, through Rank RX Holdings Limited, is entitled to a share in the annual combined profits before taxation of all the associated companies owned jointly with Xerox Corporation. This share amounts to one half of such profits up to a maximum annual sum of £3,700,627 plus one third of the amount by which such profits exceed £7,401,254, from which is deducted the related taxation.
For this purpose, the combined profits before taxation are calculated after making such adjustments as are necessary to eliminate charges made by Xerox Corporation for research and development and corporate overhead costs and the effect of inter-group trading.

38

15 Share capital and reserves

Share capital

| | 1980 | | 1979 | |
	Authorised	Issued and fully paid	Authorised	Issued and fully paid
	£000	£000	£000	£000
6½% Cumulative Preference Shares of £1 each	10,000	9,996	10,000	9,996
8% Second Cumulative Preference Shares of £1 each	3,000	2,602	3,000	2,602
Ordinary Shares of 25p each	57,000	50,498	57,000	50,339
	70,000	63,096	70,000	62,937

At 31st October 1980 4,132,549 of the unissued Ordinary shares were reserved against conversions of the outstanding 4½% Convertible Loan 1993.

Reserves

| | Group | | Company | |
	1980	1979	1980	1979
	£000	£000	£000	£000
Share premium account	141,608	140,621	141,608	140,621
Investment property revaluation reserve	36,270	2,398	—	—
Other reserves	284,558	275,160	48,832	71,815
	462,436	418,179	190,440	212,436

Movements in share capital, share premium account and investment property revaluation reserve	Issued ordinary share capital	Share premium account	Investment property revaluation reserve
	£000	£000	£000
Balances at 31st October 1979	50,339	140,621	2,398
Exchange adjustment	—	—	(368)
Issue of Ordinary Shares	159	987	—
Surplus on revaluation of investment properties	—	—	34,597
Goodwill attributable to investment properties	—	—	(357)
	50,498	141,608	36,270

| **Movements in other reserves** | Group | | | Company |
	Company and its subsidiaries	Associated companies	Total	
	£000	£000	£000	£000
Balances at 31st October 1979	87,581	187,579	275,160	71,815
Exchange adjustments	(3,595)	(1,882)	(5,477)	32
Surplus on revaluation of fixed assets	—	442	442	—
Sundry	(349)	148	(201)	—
Profit retained	(8,438)	23,072	14,634	(23,015)
Balances at 31st October 1980	75,199	209,359*	284,558	48,832
Regarded as available for distribution	66,428	—	66,428	42,113

*Includes £188,962,000 in respect of Rank Xerox Companies

39

Notes to the Accounts

16 Loan capital and borrowed money	Group		Company	
	1980	1979	1980	1979
	£000	£000	£000	£000
Bank overdrafts	8,096	8,422	—	—
Bank loans				
Amounts repayable				
Within one year or on demand	16,511	14,688	14,518	13,377
Between one and two years	633	6,158	—	5,999
Between two and five years	24,344	23,303	14,667	14,750
In five years or more	11,335	9,673	11,333	6,000
	52,823	53,822	40,518	40,126
Other borrowings				
4¼% Convertible Loan 1993	24,638	30,277	24,638	30,277
Remainder				
Amounts repayable				
Within one year	4,415	3,041	1,029	1,206
Between one and two years	21,341	9,042	1,029	1,205
Between two and five years	24,148	37,985	3,088	3,614
Between five and fifteen years	23,226	21,977	8,843	7,419
In fifteen years or more	31,207	35,694	18,736	21,097
	128,975	138,016	57,363	64,818
Total	189,894	200,260	97,881	104,944
Secured				
Sterling	26,687	27,612	16	19
Other currencies	11,147	11,423	—	—
	37,834	39,035	16	19
Unsecured				
Sterling	56,563	51,876	56,412	49,164
Other currencies	95,497	109,349	41,453	55,761
	152,060	161,225	97,865	104,925
Total as above	189,894	200,260	97,881	104,944
Deduct: Parallel loans	10,290	10,290	—	—
	179,604	189,970	97,881	104,944
Deduct: Amounts repayable within one year or on demand included in current liabilities	29,023	26,151	15,547	14,583
	150,581	163,819	82,334	90,361

Other borrowings shown above, other than the 4¼% Convertible Loan 1993, include borrowings not fully repayable within five years totalling £64,285,000 (1979 £74,631,000) for the Group and £32,725,000 (1979 £34,540,000) for the Company. These borrowings are repayable in part by annual sinking funds or by instalments and are all repayable at par. The average rate of interest payable on these borrowings was, for the Group 9.1% (1979 8.7%) and for the Company 9.3% (1979 9.5%).

Holders of the 4¼% Convertible Loan 1993 have the right to convert into fully paid Ordinary shares of the Company exercisable until 12th February 1993 on the basis of U.S. $14.523 of the Loan for one Ordinary share of 25p each. No conversion rights had been exercised by 31st October 1980 at which date U.S. $60,017,000 nominal of the loan was outstanding. During the year the Company purchased and cancelled U.S. $2,975,000 of the loan.

In 1976, a subsidiary entered into two parallel loan agreements with an overseas third party. Under each agreement the subsidiary initially borrowed U.S. $10,000,000 and lent the third party the sterling equivalent thereof. At 31st October 1980, the amount outstanding under these agreements totalled U.S. $22,949,000 (1979 U.S. $22,949,000) by the subsidiary and £10,290,000 (1979 £10,290,000) by the third party.

40

17 Deferred taxation

	Group		Company		Potential liability to deferred taxation (See note 1 (x) on page 30)			
					Group		Company	
	1980	1979	1980	1979	1980	1979	1980	1979
	£000	£000	£000	£000	£000	£000	£000	£000
Capital allowances	3,406	2,294	465	639	38,517	30,885	8,727	7,213
Stock appreciation relief	364	1,178	—	116	8,310	7,186	733	604
Other timing differences	2,226	2,578	1,713	1,587	(4,309)	(5,194)	(605)	(1,197)
Losses	—	—	—	—	(1,077)	(1,405)	—	—
	5,996	6,050	2,178	2,342	41,441	31,472	8,855	6,620
Advance corporation tax	(2,299)	(833)	—	(831)	(3,975)	(833)	(1,676)	(831)
	3,697	5,217	2,178	1,511	37,466	30,639	7,179	5,789

The above figures exclude taxation payable:
(a) in the event of profits of certain overseas subsidiary and associated companies being distributed and
(b) on capital gains estimated at £22 million (1979 £15 million) at current rates of taxation which might arise from the sale of properties at the values at which they are stated in the Group Balance Sheet.

18 Net current assets (liabilities)

	Group		Company	
	1980	1979	1980	1979
	£000	£000	£000	£000
Current assets				
Stocks				
Raw materials and work in progress	41,258	39,317	—	—
Finished goods and other stocks	62,756	62,087	3,884	3,365
Film productions	4,965	8,785	4,579	7,906
	108,979	110,189	8,463	11,271
Debtors and prepayments	105,156	94,368	3,330	3,347
Loans to Trustees of the Executive Incentive Scheme (after provisions of £37,000, 1979 £121,000 for the Group and £37,000, 1979 £70,000 for the Company)	22	71	22	46
Dividends receivable from associated companies	10,782	11,263	—	—
Short term deposits	6,682	28,138	2,000	25,676
Cash at bank and in hand	10,636	8,209	7,310	4,767
	242,257	252,238	21,125	45,107
Current liabilities				
Amount of loan capital and borrowed money repayable within one year or on demand	29,023	26,151	15,547	14,583
Creditors, provisions and accrued expenses	131,358	120,102	18,924	20,013
Acceptances by banks	25,427	22,913	—	—
United Kingdom corporation tax	1,170	3,280	—	—
Overseas taxation	2,396	1,724	—	—
Dividends				
Accrued on preference shares	194	194	194	194
Payable and proposed on Ordinary Shares	21,815	21,747	21,815	21,747
Minority shareholders of subsidiaries	1,818	1,391	—	—
	213,201	197,502	56,480	56,537
Net current assets/(liabilities)	29,056	54,736	(35,355)	(11,430)

41

19 Contingent liabilities

A claim for damages arising out of the 1975 Offer for Sale remains outstanding. The damages claimed, apart from interest, are under £600,000. The Company is advised that it has a good defence to the claim and accordingly no provision has been made.
In addition there are the following items:

Group There are contingent liabilities in respect of (a) guarantees amounting in aggregate to approximately £9,800,000 (1979 £16,700,000) including £300,000 (1979 £300,000) relating to advances by third parties at 31st October 1980 to associated companies and (b) additional taxation payable in the event of the profits of certain overseas subsidiary and associated companies being distributed.

Company There are contingent liabilities mainly in respect of advances by third parties at 31st October 1980 to (a) subsidiaries amounting in aggregate to approximately £79,400,000 (1979 £90,600,000) of which £78,000,000 (1979 £88,800,000) is included as liabilities in the Group balance sheet and (b) associated companies of approximately £300,000 (1979 £300,000).

The Company is included in a normal group value added tax registration. Companies within the group registration are jointly and severally liable for the total value added tax due by such group. At 31st October 1980 the contingent liability under these arrangements amounted to £5,199,000 (1979 £5,388,000).

20 Emoluments of Directors of The Rank Organisation Limited

			In respect of services as Directors		Other emoluments	
			1980 £000	1979 £000	1980 £000	1979 £000
Chairman			—	—	45	38
Highest paid Director			—	—	61	52
Other Directors	Number of Directors					
	1980	1979				
Nil— £5,000	6	7				
£5,001—£10,000	3	1				
£25,001—£30,000	—	1	64	43	145	117
£30,001—£35,000	—	1				
£35,001—£40,000	2	2				
£40,001—£45,000	2	—				
			64	43	251	207
Contributions to pension schemes			—	—	98	65
Pension paid to former director			—	—	6	3
Total Emoluments			64	43	355	275

21 United Kingdom employees receiving remuneration of more than £20,000

	Number of employees	
	1980	1979
£20,001—£25,000	27	10
£25,001—£30,000	7	3
£30,001—£35,000	4	—

42

Current Cost Accounts

Group Profit and Loss Account for the year ended 31st October 1980

	Note	£million	£million
Turnover			596·7
Historical cost trading profit before interest			37·2
Less Current cost operating adjustments	2		(23·2)
Current cost operating profit			14·0
Gearing adjustment		4·9	
Interest on net borrowing	3	(22·0)	(17·1)
			(3·1)
Associated Companies			
Per historical cost accounts		96·0	
Less Current cost adjustments	4	(22·6)	73·4
Current cost profit before taxation			70·3
Taxation			(50·0)
			20·3
Minority interests			(3·7)
Profit before extraordinary items			16·6
Extraordinary items			(20·9)
Current cost loss attributable to The Rank Organisation Limited			(4·3)
Dividends			(22·4)
Current cost deficit for the year			(26·7)

Notes to the current cost accounts (CCA)
1. Accounting policies

(a) CCA are based on historical cost accounts adjusted to comply with SSAP 16. Investment properties have not been adjusted. Lack of CCA information for some overseas subsidiaries is not believed material to this presentation. CCA figures allow for price changes specific to the business.
As this is the first year for which full CCA figures are presented, comparative figures are not shown.

(b) The gross current cost of fixed assets had been derived as follows:—
Plant has been restated using appropriate Government indices applied to the historical costs. The current cost of land and non-specialised buildings has been estimated by the Directors based upon the advice of executives of the Group who hold appropriate professional qualifications. The valuations adopted for these purposes have in certain cases been taken to be equal to the depreciated net book amount as reflected in the historical cost accounts, principally in respect of theatre properties.

(c) Other accounting policies:
Except as set out above the policies used in the current cost accounts are the same as those used in the historical cost accounts.

2. Current cost operating adjustments

	£m
Cost of sales	(8·9)
Monetary working capital	(0·7)
	(9·6)
Depreciation	(13·0)
Fixed asset disposals	(0·6)
	(23·2)

3. Gearing adjustment
In calculating the gearing adjustment,
(a) shareholders' funds have been adjusted to eliminate from the balance sheet, investments, goodwill and the net interest in investment properties, and
(b) average borrowings during the year of £82·2 million have been attributed to investment properties.

Notes continue on page 44.

43

97

Group Balance Sheet as at 31st October 1980

	Note	£million	£million
Assets employed			
Fixed assets			
Investment properties			156·1
Other fixed assets	5		446·6
Investments			297·7
Goodwill			34·1
Working capital			
Stock		110·5	
Trade creditors less trade debtors		(26·2)	84·3
Net operating assets			1,018·8
Financed by			
Ordinary share capital			50·5
Reserves: Current cost	6		288·1
Other			421·1
Ordinary shareholders' funds			759·7
Preference share capital			12·6
Minority interests			39·5
Dividends payable			21·8
Total shareholders' interest			833·6
Net borrowing			
Loan capital and borrowed money		150·6	
Deferred taxation		3·7	
Other current liabilities/assets (net)		30·9	185·2
			1,018·8

Notes to the current cost accounts (CCA) (continued)

4. Associated companies: current cost adjustments	£m
Cost of sales	(6·1)
Monetary working capital	(3·6)
	(9·7)
Depreciation	(13·1)
Fixed asset disposals	(1·1)
	(23·9)
Foreign currency translation	(4·3)
Gearing adjustment	5·6
	(22·6)

6. Current cost reserve	£m
Balance at 1st November 1979	230·2
Revaluation surpluses reflecting price changes:	
Land and buildings	46·6
Plant and machinery	13·2
Stock	8·2
Investments	(4·3)
Monetary working capital adjustment	0·7
Gearing adjustment	(4·9)
Minority interests	(1·5)
Balance at 31st October 1980	288·1
of which: Realised	41·3
Unrealised	246·8
	288·1

5. Other fixed assets	Gross current replacement cost or valuation £m	Depreciation £m	Net current replacement cost or valuation £m
Freehold land and buildings	276·3	35·7	240·6
Leasehold land and buildings	110·4	13·1	97·3
Plant, vehicles and equipment	261·5	152·8	108·7
44	648·2	201·6	446·6

CAS Occasional Papers

Civil Service College Occasional Papers

Civil Service College Handbooks

No

1	The design of information-processing systems for government	J H Robertson
2	Flow-charts, logical trees and algorithms for rules and regulations	B N Lewis, I S Horabin and C P Gane
3	Network analysis in forming a new organisation	W S Ryan
4	Output budgeting and the contribution of micro-economics to efficiency in government	Alan Williams
5	Input-output analysis and its application to education and manpower planning	P Redfern
6	The elementary ideas of game theory	Maurice Peston and Alan Coddington
7	Statistical decision theory	Maurice Peston and Alan Coddington

Printed in England for Her Majesty's Stationery Office
by Hobbs the Printers of Southampton
(2037) Dd716735 C50 1/82 G381

100